Elements of Foreign Exchange

by Franklin Escher

CONTENTS

PAGE

CHAPTER I.

WHAT FOREIGN EXCHANGE IS AND WHAT BRINGS IT INTO EXIST 3

The various forms of obligation between the bankers and merchants of one country and the bankers and merchants of another, which result in the drawing of bills of exchange.

CHAPTER II.

THE DEMAND FOR BILLS OF EXCHANGE 15

A discussion of the six sources from which spring the demand for the various kinds of bills of exchange.

CHAPTER III.

THE RISE AND FALL OF EXCHANGE RATES 25

Operation of the five main influences tending to make exchange rise as opposed to the five main influences tending to make exchange fall.

CHAPTER IV.

THE VARIOUS KINDS OF EXCHANGE 45

A detailed description of: Commercial "Long" Bills--Clean Bills--Commercial "Short" Bills--Drafts drawn against securities sold abroad--Bankers' demand drafts--Bankers' "long" drafts.

CHAPTER V.

THE FOREIGN EXCHANGE MARKET 59

How the exchange market is constituted. The bankers, dealers and brokers who make it up. How exchange rates are established. The relative importance of different kinds of exchange.

CHAPTER VI.

HOW MONEY IS MADE IN FOREIGN EXCHANGE. THE OPERATIONS OF THE FOREIGN DEPARTMENT 68

An intimate description of: Selling demand bills against remittances of demand bills--Selling cables against remittances of demand bills--Selling demand drafts against remittances of "long" exchange--The operation of lending foreign money here--The drawing of finance bills--Arbitraging in Foreign Exchange--Dealing in exchange "futures."

CHAPTER VII.

GOLD EXPORTS AND IMPORTS 106

The primary movement of gold from the mines to the markets, and its subsequent distribution along the lines of favorable exchange rates. Description (with presentation of actual figures) of: The export of gold bars from New York to London--Import of gold bars from London--Export of gold bars to Paris under the "triangular operation." Shipments to Argentina.

London as a "free" gold market and the ability of the Central Banks in Europe to control the movement of gold.

CHAPTER VIII.

FOREIGN EXCHANGE IN ITS RELATION TO INTERNATIONAL SECURITY TRADING 130

Europe's "fixed" and "floating" investment in American bonds and stocks a constant source of international security trading. Consequent foreign exchange business. Financing foreign speculation in "Americans." Description of the various kinds of bond and stock "arbitrage."

CHAPTER IX.

THE FINANCING OF EXPORTS AND IMPORTS 141

A complete description of the international banking system by which merchandise is imported into and exported from the United States. An actual operation followed through its successive steps.

PREFACE

"Where can I find a little book from which I can get a clear idea of how foreign exchange works, without going too deeply into it?"--that question, put to the author dozens of times and by many different kinds of people, is responsible for the existence of this little work. There are one or two well-written textbooks on foreign exchange, but never yet has the author come across a book which covered this subject in such a way that the man who knew little or nothing about it could pick up the book and within a few hours get a clear idea of how foreign exchange works,--the causes which bear upon its movement, its influence on the money and security markets, etc.

That is the object of this little book--to cover the ground of foreign exchange, but in such a way as to make the subject interesting and its treatment readable and comprehensible to the man without technical knowledge. Foreign exchange is no easy subject to understand; there are few important subjects which are. But, on the other hand, neither is it the complicated and abstruse subject which so many people seem to consider it--an idea only too often born of a look into some of the textbooks on exchange, with their formidable pages of tabulations, formulas, and calculations of all descriptions. For the average man there is little of interest in these intricacies of the subject. Many of the shrewdest and most successful exchange bankers in New York City, indeed, know less about them than do some of their clerks. What is needed is rather a clear and definite knowledge of the movement of exchange--why it moves as it does, what can be read from its movements, what effects its movements exert on the other markets. It is in the hope that something may be added to the general understanding of these important matters that this little book is offered to the public.

THE ELEMENTS OF FOREIGN EXCHANGE

CHAPTER I

WHAT FOREIGN EXCHANGE IS AND WHAT BRINGS IT INTO EXISTENCE

Underlying the whole business of foreign exchange is the way in which obligations between creditors in one country and debtors in another have come to be settled--by having the creditor draw a draft directly upon the debtor or upon some bank designated by him. A merchant in New York has sold a bill of goods to a merchant in London, having thus become his creditor, say, for $5,000. To get his money, the merchant in New York will, in the great majority of cases, draw a sterling draft upon the debtor in London for a little over ?,000. This draft his banker will readily enough convert for him into dollars. The buying and selling and discounting of countless such bills of exchange constitute the very foundation of the foreign exchange business.

Not all international obligations are settled by having the creditor draw direct on the debtor. Sometimes gold is actually sent in payment. Sometimes the debtor goes to a banker engaged in selling drafts on the city where the obligation exists, gets such a draft from him and sends that. But in the vast majority of cases payment is effected as stated--by a draft drawn directly on the buyer of the goods. John Smith in London owes me money. I draw on him for ?00, take the draft around to my bank and sell it at, say, 4.86, getting for it a check for $486.00. I have my money, and I am out of the transaction.

Obligations continually arising in the course of trade and finance between firms in New York and firms in London, it follows that every day in New York there will be merchants with sterling drafts on London which they are anxious to sell for dollars, and vice versa. The supply of exchange, therefore, varies with the obligations of one country to another. If merchants in New York, for instance, have sold goods in quantity in London, a great many drafts on London will be drawn and offered for sale in the New York exchange market. The supply, it will of course be apparent, varies. Sometimes there are many drafts for sale; sometimes very few. When there are a great many drafts offering, their makers will naturally have to accept a lower rate of exchange than when the supply is light.

The par of exchange between any two countries is the price of the gold unit of one expressed in the money of the other. Take England and the United States. The gold unit of England is the pound sterling. What is the price of as much gold as there is in a new pound sterling, expressed in American money? $4.8665. That amount of dollars and cents at any United States assay office will buy exactly as much gold as there is contained in a new British pound sterling, or sovereign, as the actual coin itself is called. 4.8665 is the mint par of exchange between Great Britain and the United States.

The fact that the gold in a new British sovereign (or pound sterling) is worth $4.8665 in our money by no means proves, however, that drafts payable in pounds in London can always be bought or sold for $4.8665 per pound. To reduce the case to a unit basis, suppose that you owed one pound in London, and that, finding it difficult to buy a draft to send in payment, you elected to send actual gold. The amount of gold necessary to settle your debt would cost $4.8665, in addition to which you would have to pay all the expenses of remitting. It would be cheaper, therefore, to pay considerably more than $4.8665 for a one-pound draft, and you would probably bid up until somebody consented to sell you the draft you wanted.

Which goes to show that the mint par is not what governs the price at which drafts in pounds sterling can be bought, but that demand and supply are the controlling factors. There are exporters who have been shipping merchandise and selling foreign exchange against the shipments all their lives who have never even heard of a mint par of exchange. All they know is, that when exports are running large and bills in great quantity are being offered, bankers are willing to pay them only low rates--$4.83 or $4.84, perhaps, for the commercial bills they want to sell for dollars. Conversely, when exports are running light and bills drawn against shipments are scarce, bankers may be willing to pay 4.87 or 4.88 for them.

For a clear understanding of the mechanics of the exchange market there is necessary a clear understanding of what the various forms of obligations are which bring foreign exchange into existence. Practically all bills originate from one of the following causes:

1. Merchandise has been shipped and the shipper draws his draft on the buyer or on a bank abroad designated by him.

2. Securities have been sold abroad and the seller is drawing on the buyer for the purchase price.

3. Foreign money is being loaned in this market, the operation necessitating the drawing of drafts on the lender.

4. Finance-bills are being drawn, i.e., a banker abroad is allowing a banker here to draw on him in pounds sterling at 60 or 90 days' sight in order that the drawer of the drafts may sell them (for dollars) and use the proceeds until the drafts come due and have to be paid.

1. Looking at these sources of supply in the order in which they are given, it is apparent, first, what a vast amount of foreign exchange originates from the direct export of merchandise from this country. Exports for the period given below have been as follows:

1913 $2,465,884,000 1912 2,204,322,000 1911 2,049,320,000 1910 1,744,984,000 1909 1,663,011,000

Not all of this merchandise is drawn against; in some cases the buyer abroad chooses rather to secure a dollar draft on some American bank and to send that in payment. But in the vast majority of cases the regular course is followed and the seller here draws on the buyer there.

There are times, therefore, when exchange originating from this source is much more plentiful than at others. During the last quarter of each year, for instance, when the cereal and cotton crop exports are at their height, exchange comes flooding into the New York market from all over the country, literally by the hundreds of millions of dollars. The natural effect is to depress rates--sometimes to a point where it becomes possible to use the cheaply obtainable exchange to buy gold on the other side.

In a following chapter a more detailed description of the New York exchange market is given, but in passing, it is well to note how the whole country's supply of commercial exchange, with certain exceptions, is focussed on New York. Chicago, Philadelphia, and one or two other large cities carry on a pretty large business in exchange, independent of New York, but by far the greater part of the commercial exchange originating throughout the country finds its way to the metropolis. For in New York are situated so many banks and bankers dealing in bills of exchange that a close market is always assured. The cotton exporter in Memphis can send the bills he has drawn on London or Liverpool to his broker in New York with the fullest assurance that they will be sold to the bankers at the highest possible rate of exchange anywhere obtainable.

2. The second source of supply is in the sale abroad of stocks and bonds. Here again it will be evident how the supply of bills must vary. There are times when heavy flotations of bonds are being made here with Europe participating largely, at which times the exchange drawn against the securities placed abroad mounts up enormously in volume. Then again there are times when London and Paris and Berlin buy heavily into our listed shares and when every mail finds the stock exchange houses here drawing millions of pounds, marks, and francs upon their correspondents abroad. At such times the supply of bills is apt to become very great.

Origin of bills from this source, too, is apt to exert an important influence on rates, in that it is often sudden and often concentrated on a comparatively short period of time. The announcement of a single big bond issue, often, where it is an assured fact that a large part of it will be placed abroad, is enough to seriously depress the exchange market. Bankers know that when the shipping abroad of the bonds begins, large amounts of bills drawn against them will be offered and that rates will in all probability be driven down.

Announcements of such issues, as well as announcements that a block of this or that kind of bonds has been placed abroad with some foreign syndicate, are apt to come suddenly and often find the exchange market unprepared. For the supply of exchange originated thereby, it must be remembered, is not confined to the amount actually drawn against bonds sold but includes also all the exchange which other bankers, in their anticipation of lower rates, hasten to draw. The exchange market is, indeed, a sensitive barometer, from which those who understand it can read all sorts of coming developments. It often happens that buying or selling movements in our securities by the foreigners are so clearly forecasted by the action of the exchange market that bankers here are able to gain great advantage from what they are able to foresee.

3. The third great source of supply is in the drafts which bankers in one country draw upon bankers in another in the operation of making international loans. The mechanism of such transactions will be treated in greater detail later on, but without any knowledge of the subject whatever, it is plain that the transfer of banking capital, say from England to the United States, can best be effected by having the American house draw upon the English bank which wants to lend the money. In the finely adjusted state of the foreign exchanges nowadays, loans are continually being made by bankers in one country to bankers and merchants in another. Very little of the capital so transferred goes in the form of gold. A London house decides to loan, say, $100,000 in the American market. The terms having been arranged, the London house cables its New York correspondent to draw for ?0,000, at 60 or 90 days' sight, as the case may be. The New York house, having drawn the draft, sells it in the exchange market, realizing on it the $100,000, which it then proceeds to loan out according to instructions.

The arranging of these loans, it will be seen, means the continuous creation of very large amounts of foreign exchange. As the financial relationships between our bankers and those of the Old World have been developed, it has come about that European money is being put out in this market in increasing volume. Conditions of money, discount, and exchange are constantly being watched for the opportunity to make loans on favorable terms, and the aggregate of foreign money loaned out here at times reaches very large figures. In 1901 Europe had big amounts of money outstanding in the New York market, and again in 1906 very large sums of English and French capital were temporarily placed at our disposal. But in the summer of 1909 all records were surpassed, American borrowings in London and Paris footing up to at least half a billion dollars. Such loans, running only a couple of months on the average and then being sometimes paid off, but more often shifted about or renewed, give rise to the drawing of immense amounts of foreign exchange.

4. Drawing of so-called "finance-bills," of which a complete description will be found in chapters IV and VI, is the fourth source whence foreign exchange originates. Whenever money rates become decidedly higher in one of the great markets than in the others, bankers at that point who have the requisite facilities and credit, arrange with bankers in other markets to allow them (the bankers at the point where money is high) to draw 60 or 90 days' sight bills. These bills can then be disposed of in the exchange market, dollars being realized on them, which can then be loaned out during the whole life of the bills. The advantages or dangers of such an operation will not be touched upon here, the purpose of this chapter being merely to set forth clearly the sources from which foreign exchange originates.

And when money is decidedly higher in New York than in London an immense volume of foreign exchange does originate from this source. A number of firms and banks, with either their own branches in London or with correspondents there to whom they stand very close, are in a position where they can draw very large amounts of finance bills whenever they deem it profitable and expedient to do so. Eventually, of course, these 60 and 90 day bills come due and have to be settled by remittances of demand exchange, but in the meantime the house which drew them will have had the unrestricted use of the money. In a market like New York this is only too often a prime consideration. With money rates soaring as they do so frequently here, a banker can pay almost any commission his correspondent abroad demands and still come out ahead on the transaction.

These are the principal sources from which foreign exchange originates-- shipments of merchandise, sales abroad of securities, transfer of foreign banking capital to this side, sale of finance-bills. Other causes of less importance--interest and profits on American capital invested in Europe, for instance--are responsible for the existence of some quantity of exchange, but the great bulk of it originates from one of the four sources above set forth. In the next chapter effort will be made to show whence arises the demand which pretty effectually absorbs all the supply of exchange produced each year.

CHAPTER II

THE DEMAND FOR BILLS OF EXCHANGE

Turning now to consideration of the various sources from which springs the demand for foreign exchange, it appears that they can be divided about as follows:

1. The need for exchange with which to pay for imports of merchandise.

2. The need for exchange with which to pay for securities (American or foreign) purchased by us in Europe.

3. The necessity of remitting abroad the interest and dividends on the huge sums of foreign capital invested here, and the money which foreigners domiciled in this country are continually sending home.

4. The necessity of remitting abroad freight and insurance money earned

here by foreign companies.

5. Money to cover American tourists' disbursements and expenses of wealthy Americans living abroad.

6. The need for exchange with which to pay off maturing foreign short-loans and finance-bills.

1. Payment for merchandise imported constitutes probably the most important source of demand for foreign exchange. Merchandise brought into the country for the period given herewith has been valued as follows:

1913 $1,813,008,000 1912 1,653,264,000 1911 1,527,226,000 1910 1,556,947,000 1909 1,311,920,000

Practically the whole amount of these huge importations has had to be paid for with bills of exchange. Whether the merchandise in question is cutlery manufactured in England or coffee grown in Brazil, the chances are it will be paid for (under a system to be described hereafter) by a bill of exchange drawn on London or some other great European financial center. From one year's end to the other there is constantly this demand for bills with which to pay for merchandise brought into the country. As in the case of exports, which are largest in the Fall, there is much more of a demand for exchange with which to pay for imports at certain times of the year than at others, but at all times merchandise in quantity is coming into the country and must be paid for with bills of exchange.

2. The second great source of demand originates out of the necessity of making payment for securities purchased abroad. So far as the American participation in foreign bond issues is concerned, the past few years have seen very great developments. We are not yet a people, as are the English or the French, who invest a large proportion of their accumulated savings outside of their own country, but as our investment surplus has increased in size, it has come about that American investors have been going in more and

more extensively for foreign bonds. There have been times, indeed, as when the Japanese loans were being floated, when very large amounts of foreign exchange were required to pay for the bonds taken by American individuals and syndicates.

Security operations involving a demand for foreign exchange are, however, by no means confined to American participation in foreign bond issues. Accumulated during the course of the past half century, there is a perfectly immense amount of American securities held all over Europe. The greater part of this investment is in bonds and remains untouched for years at a stretch. But then there come times when, for one reason or another, waves of selling pass over the European holdings of "Americans," and we are required to take back millions of dollars' worth of our stocks and bonds. Such selling movements do not really get very far below the surface--they do not, for instance, disturb the great blocks of American bonds in which so large a proportion of many of the big foreign fortunes are invested, but they are apt to be, nevertheless, on a scale which requires large amounts of exchange to pay for what we have had to buy back.

The same thing is true with stocks, though in that case the selling movements are more frequent and less important. Europe is always interested heavily in American stocks, there being, as in the case of bonds, a big fixed investment of capital, beside a continually fluctuating "floating-investment." In other words, aside from their fixed investments in our stocks, the foreigners are continually speculating in them and continually changing their position as buyers and sellers. Selling movements such as these do not materially affect Europe's set position on our stocks, but they do result at times in very large amounts of our stocks being dumped back upon us--sometimes when we are ready for them, sometimes when the operation is decidedly painful, as in the Fall of 1907. In any case, when Europe sells, we buy. And when we buy, and at the rate of millions of dollars' worth a day, there is a big demand for exchange with which to pay for what we have bought.

3. So great is the foreign investment of capital in this country that the necessity of remitting the interest and dividends alone means another continuous demand for very large amounts of foreign exchange. Estimates of how much European money is invested here are little better than guesses. The only sure thing about it is that the figures run well up into the billions and that several hundred millions of dollars' worth of interest and dividends must be sent across the water each year. There are, in the first place, all the foreign investments in what might be called private enterprise--the English money, for instance, invested in fruit orchards, gold and copper mines, etc., in the western states. Profits on this money are practically all remitted back to England, but no way exists of even estimating what they amount to. Aside from that there are all the foreign holdings of bonds and stocks in our great public corporations, holdings whose ownership it is impossible to trace. Only at the interest periods at the beginning and middle of each year does it become apparent how large a proportion of our bonds are held in Europe and how great is the demand for exchange with which to make the remittances of accrued interest. At such times the incoming mails of the international banking houses bulge with great quantities of coupons sent over here for collection. For several weeks on either side of the two important interest periods, the exchange market feels the stimulus of the demand for exchange with which the proceeds of these masses of coupons are to be sent abroad.

4. Freights and insurance are responsible for a fourth important source of demand for foreign exchange. A walk along William Street in New York is all that is necessary to give a good idea of the number and importance of the foreign companies doing business in the United States. In some form or other all the premiums paid have to be sent to the other side. Times come, of course, like the year of the Baltimore fire, when losses by these foreign companies greatly outbalance premiums received, the business they do thus resulting in the actual creation of great amounts of foreign exchange, but in the long run--year in, year out--the remitting abroad of the premiums earned means a steady demand for exchange.

With freights it is the same proposition, except that the proportion of

American shipping business done by foreign companies is much greater than the proportion of insurance business done by foreign companies. Since the Civil War the American mercantile marine instead of growing with the country has gone steadily backward, until now the greater part of our shipping is done in foreign bottoms. Aside from the other disadvantages of such a condition, the payment of such great sums for freight to foreign companies is a direct economic drain. An estimate that the yearly freight bill amounts to $150,000,000 is probably not too high. That means that in the course of every year there is a demand for that amount of exchange with which to remit back what has been earned from us.

5. Tourists' expenditures abroad are responsible for a further heavy demand for exchange. Whether it is because Americans are fonder of travel than the people of other countries or whether it is because of our more or less isolated position on the map, it is a fact that there are far more Americans traveling about in Europe than people belonging to any other nation. And the sums spent by American tourists in foreign lands annually aggregate a very large amount--possibly as much as $175,000,000--all of which has eventually to be covered by remittances of exchange from this side.

Then again there must be considered the expenditures of wealthy Americans who either live abroad entirely or else spend a large part of their time on the other side. During the past decade it has come about that every European city of any consequence has its "American Colony," a society no longer composed of poor art students or those whose residence abroad is not a matter of volition, but consisting now of many of the wealthiest Americans. By these expatriates money is spent extremely freely, their drafts on London and Paris requiring the frequent replenishment, by remittances of exchange from this side, of their bank balances at those points. Furthermore, there must be considered the great amounts of American capital transferred abroad by the marriage of wealthy American women with titled foreigners. Such alliances mean not only the transfer of large amounts of capital en bloc, but mean as well, usually, an annual remittance of a very large sum of money. No account of the money drained out of the country in this way is kept, of course, but it is an item which certainly runs up into the tens of millions.

6. Lastly, there is the demand for exchange originating from the paying off of the short-term loans which European bankers so continuously make in the American market. There is never a time nowadays when London and Paris are lending American bankers less than $100,000,000 on 60 or 90 day bills, while the total frequently runs up to three or four times that amount. The sum of these floating loans is, indeed, changing all the time, a circumstance which in itself is responsible for a demand for very great amounts of foreign exchange.

Take, for instance, the amount of French and English capital employed in this market in the form of short-term loans; $250,000,000 is probably a fair estimate of the average amount, and 90 days a fair estimate of the average time the loans run before being paid off or renewed. That means that the quarter of a billion dollars of floating indebtedness is "turned over" four times a year and that means that every year the rearrangement of these loans gives rise to a demand for a billion dollars' worth of foreign exchange. These loaning operations, it must be understood, both originate exchange and create a demand for it. They are mentioned, therefore, in the preceding chapter, as one of the sources from which exchange originates, and now as one of the sources from which, during the course of every year, springs a demand for a very great quantity of exchange.

The six sources of demand for exchange, then, are for the payment for imports; for securities purchased abroad; for the remitting abroad of interest on foreign capital invested here and the money which foreigners in this country send home; for remitting freight and insurance profits earned by foreign companies here; for tourists' expenses abroad; and lastly, for the paying off of foreign loans. From these sources spring practically all the demand for exchange. In the last chapter there were set forth the principal sources of supply. With a clear understanding of where exchange comes from and of where it goes, it ought now to be possible for the student of the subject to grasp the causes which bear on the movement of exchange rates. That subject will accordingly be taken up in the next chapter.

CHAPTER III

THE RISE AND FALL OF EXCHANGE RATES

Granted that the obligations to each other of any two given countries foot up to the same amount, it is evident that the rate of exchange will remain exactly at the gold par--that in New York, for instance, the price of the sovereign will be simply the mint value of the gold contained in the sovereign. But between no two countries does such a condition exist--take any two, and the amount of the obligation of one to the other changes every day, which causes a continuous fluctuation in the exchange rate--sometimes up from the mint par, sometimes down.

Before going on to discuss the various causes influencing the movement of exchange rates, there is one point which should be very clearly understood. Two countries, at least, are concerned in the fluctuation of every rate. Take, for example, London and New York, and assume that, at New York, exchange on London is falling. That in itself means that, in London, exchange on New York is rising.

For the sake of clearness, in the ensuing discussion of the influences tending to raise and lower exchange rates, New York is chosen as the point at which these influences are operative. Consideration will be given first to the influences which cause exchange to go up. In a general way, it will be noticed, they conform with the sources of demand for exchange given in the previous chapter. They may be classified about as follows:

1. Large imports, calling for large amounts of exchange with which to make the necessary payments.

2. Large purchases of foreign securities by us, or repurchase of our own securities abroad, calling for large amounts of exchange with which to make payment.

3. Coming to maturity of issues of American bonds held abroad.

4. Low money rates here, which result in a demand for exchange with which to send banking capital out of the country.

5. High money rates at some foreign centre which create a great demand for exchange drawn on that centre.

1. Heavy imports are always a potent factor in raising the level of exchange rates. Under whatever financial arrangement or from whatever point merchandise is imported into the United States, payment is almost invariably made by draft on London, Paris, or Berlin. At times when imports run especially heavy, demand from importers for exchange often outweighs every other consideration, forcing rates up to high levels. A practical illustration is to be found in the inpour of merchandise which took place just before the tariff legislation in 1909. Convinced that duties were to be raised, importers rushed millions of dollars' worth of merchandise of every description into the country. The result was that the demand for exchange became so great that in spite of the fact that it was the season when exports normally meant low exchange, rates were pushed up to the gold export point.

2. Heavy purchasing movements of our own or foreign securities, on the other side, are the second great influence making for high exchange. There come times when, for one reason or another, the movement of securities is all one way, and when it happens that for any cause we are the ones who are doing the buying, the exchange market is likely to be sharply influenced upward by the demand for bills with which to make payments. Such movements on a greater or less scale go on all the time and constitute one of the principal factors which exchange managers take into consideration in making their estimate of possible exchange market fluctuations.

It is interesting, for instance, to note the movement of foreign exchange at times when a heavy selling movement of American stocks by the foreigners is under way. Origin of security-selling on the Stock Exchange is by no means easy to trace, but there are times when the character of the brokers doing the selling and the very nature of the stocks being disposed of mean much to the experienced eye. Take, for instance, a day when half a dozen brokers usually identified with the operations of the international houses are consistently selling such stocks as Missouri, Kansas & Texas, Baltimore & Ohio, or Canadian Pacific--whether or not the inference that the selling is for foreign account is correct can very probably be read from the movement of the exchange market. If it is the case that the selling comes from abroad and that we are buying, large orders for foreign exchange are almost certain to make their appearance and to give the market a very strong tone if not actually to urge it sharply upward. Such orders are not likely to be handled in a way which makes them apparent to everybody, but as a rule it is impossible to execute them without creating a condition in the exchange market apparent to every shrewd observer. And, as a matter of fact, many an operation in the international stocks is based upon judgment as to what the action of the exchange market portends. Similarly--the other way around-- exchange managers very frequently operate in exchange on the strength of what they judge or know is going to happen in the market for the international stocks. With the exchange market sensitive to developments, knowledge that there is to be heavy selling in some quarter of the stock market, from abroad, is almost equivalent to knowledge of a coming sharp rise in exchange on London.

Perhaps the best illustration of how exchange can be affected by foreign selling of our securities occurred just after the beginning of the panic period in October of 1907. Under continuous withdrawals of New York capital from the foreign markets, exchange had sold down to a very low point. Suddenly came the memorable selling movement of "Americans" by English and German investors. Within two or three days perhaps a million shares of American stocks were jettisoned in this market by the foreigners, while exchange rose by leaps and bounds nearly 10 cents to the pound, to the unheard-of price of 4.91. Nobody had exchange to sell and almost overnight there had been created a demand for tens of millions of dollars' worth.

3. The coming to maturity of American bonds held abroad is another influencing factor closely kept track of by dealers in exchange. So extensive is the total foreign investment in American bonds that issues are coming due all the time. Where some especially large issue runs off without being funded with new bonds, demand for exchange often becomes very strong. Especially is this the case with the short-term issues of the railroads and most especially with New York City revenue warrants which have become so exceedingly popular a form of investment among the foreign bankers. In spite of its mammoth debt, New York City is continually putting out revenue warrants, the operation amounting, in fact, to the issue of its notes. Of late years Paris bankers, especially, have found the discounting of these "notes" a profitable operation and have at times taken them in big blocks.

Whenever one of these blocks of revenue warrants matures and has to be paid off, the exchange market is likely to be strongly affected. Accumulation of exchange in preparation is likely to be carried on for some weeks ahead, but even at that the resulting steady demand for bills often exerts a decidedly stimulating influence. Experienced exchange managers know at all times just what short-term issues are coming due, about what proportion of the bonds or notes have found their way to the other side, just how far ahead the exchange is likely to be accumulated. Repayment operations of this kind are often almost a dominant, though usually temporary, influence on the price of exchange.

4. Low money rates are the fourth great factor influencing foreign exchange upward. Whenever money is cheap at any given center, and borrowers are bidding only low rates for its use, lenders seek a more profitable field for the employment of their capital. It has come about during the past few years that so far as the operation of loaning money is concerned, the whole financial world is one great market, New York bankers nowadays loaning out their money in London with the same facility with which they used to loan it out in Boston or Philadelphia. So close have become the financial relationships between leading banking houses in New York and London that the slightest

opportunity for profitable loaning operations is immediately availed of.

Money rates in the New York market are not often less attractive than those in London, so that American floating capital is not generally employed in the English market, but it does occasionally come about that rates become abnormally low here and that bankers send away their balances to be loaned out at other points. During long periods of low money, indeed, it often happens that large lending institutions here send away a considerable part of their deposits, to be steadily employed for loaning out and discounting bills in some foreign market. Such a time was the long period of stagnant money conditions following the 1907 panic. Trust companies and banks who were paying interest on large deposits at that time sent very large amounts of money to the other side and kept big balances running with their correspondents at such points as Amsterdam, Copenhagen, St. Petersburg, etc.,--anywhere, in fact, where some little demand for money actually existed. Demand for exchange with which to send this money abroad was a big factor in keeping exchange rates at their high level during all that long period.

5. High money rates at some given foreign point as a factor in elevating exchange rates on that point might almost be considered as a corollary of low money here, but special considerations often govern such a condition and make it worth while to note its effect. Suppose, for instance, that at a time when money market conditions all over the world are about normal, rates, for any given reason, begin to rise at some point, say London. Instantly a flow of capital begins in that direction. In New York, Paris, Berlin and other centers it is realized that London is bidding better rates for money than are obtainable locally, and bankers forthwith make preparations to increase the sterling balances they are employing in London. Exchange on that particular point being in such demand, rates begin to rise, and continue to rise, according to the urgency of the demand.

Particular attention will be given later on to the way in which the Bank of England and the other great foreign banks manipulate the money market and so control the course of foreign exchange upon themselves, but in passing it is well to note just why it is that when the interest rate at any given point begins to go up, foreign exchange drawn upon that point begins to go up, too. Remittances to the point where the better bid for money is being made, are the very simple explanation. Bankers want to send money there, and to do it they need bills of exchange. An urgent enough demand inevitably means a rise in the quotation at which the bills are obtainable. Which suggests very plainly why it is that when the Directors of the Bank of England want to raise the rate of exchange upon London, at New York or Paris or Berlin, they go about it by tightening up the English money market.

The foregoing are the principal causes making for high exchange. The causes which make up for low rates must necessarily be to a certain extent merely the converse, but for the sake of clearness they are set down. The division is about as follows:

1. Especially heavy exports of merchandise.

2. Large purchases of our stocks by the foreigners and the placing abroad of blocks of American bonds.

3. Distrust on our part of financial conditions existing at some point abroad where there are carried large deposits of American capital.

4. High money rates here.

5. Unprofitably low loaning rates at some important foreign centre where American bankers ordinarily carry large balances on deposit.

1. Just as unusually large imports of commodities mean a sharp demand for exchange with which to pay for them, unusually large exports mean a big supply of bills. In a previous chapter it has been explained how, when merchandise is shipped out of the country, the shipper draws his draft upon the buyer, in the currency of the country to which the merchandise goes. When exports are heavy, therefore, a great volume of bills of exchange drawn

in various kinds of currency comes on the market for sale, naturally depressing rates.

Exports continue on a certain scale all through the year, but, like imports, are heavier at some times than others. In the Fall, for instance, when the year's crops are being exported, shipments out of the country invariably reach their zenith, the export nadir being approached in midsummer, when the crop has been mostly exported and shipments of manufactured goods are running light.

From the middle of August, when the first of the new cotton crop begins to find its way to the seaport, until the middle of December, when the bulk of the corn and wheat crop exports have been completed, exchange in very great volume finds its way into the New York market. Normally this is the season of low rates, for which reason many shippers of cotton and grain, who know months in advance approximately how much they will ship, contract ahead of time with exchange dealers in New York for the sale of the bills they know they will have. By so doing, shippers are often able to obtain very much better rates. They can then protect themselves, at least, from the extremely low rates which they may be forced to take if they wait and accept going rates at a time when shippers all over the country are trying to sell their bills at the same time.

How great is the rush of exchange into market may be seen from the statistics of cotton exports during the period given below. Not all of this cotton goes out during the last four months of the year, but the greater part of it does and, furthermore, cotton, while the most important, is only one of the domestic products exported in the autumn.

MONEY VALUE OF COTTON EXPORTED

1913 $547,357,000 1912 565,849,000 1911 585,318,000 1910 450,447,000 1909 417,390,000

During the autumn months, under normal conditions, the advantage is all with the buyer of foreign exchange. By every mail huge packages of bills, drawn against shipments of cotton, wheat and corn, come pouring into the New York market. Bankers' portfolios become crowded with bills; remittances by each steamer, in the case of some of the big bankers, run up, literally, into the millions of dollars. Naturally, any one wanting bankers' exchange is usually able to secure it at a low price.

2. With regard to the second influence making for low exchange, sale of American bonds or stocks abroad, no season can be set when the influence is more likely to be operative than at any other, unless, possibly, it be the Spring, when money rates are more apt to be low and bond issues larger than at any other time of the year. No time, however, can be definitely set--there are years when the bulk of the new issues are brought out in the Spring and other years when the Fall season sees most of the new financing. But whatever the time of the year, one thing is certain--the issue of any amount of American bonds with Europe participating largely means a full supply of foreign exchange not only during the time the issues are actually being brought out, but for long afterward.

There used to be a saying among exchange dealers that cotton exports make exchange faster than anything, but nowadays bond sales abroad have come to take first place. For foreign participation in syndicates formed to underwrite new issues almost invariably means the drawing of bills representing the full amount of the foreign participation. A syndicate is formed, for instance, to take off the hands of the X Y Z railroad $30,000,000 of new bonds, the arrangement being that the railroad is to receive its money at once and that the syndicate is to take its own time about working off the bonds. Half the amount, say, has been allotted to foreign houses. Immediately, the drawing of ?,000,000, or francs 75,000,000, as the case may be, begins. The foreign houses have to raise the money, and in nine cases out of ten, their way of doing it is to arrange with some representative abroad to let them draw long drafts, against the deposit of securities on this side. These drafts, in pounds or francs, at sixty to ninety days' sight, they can sell in the exchange market for dollars, thus securing the money they have agreed to turn over to the railroad. In the meantime, during the life of the drafts they have set afloat and before they come due and have to be paid off, the bankers here can go about selling the bonds and getting back their money. Perhaps before the sixty or ninety days, as the case may be, are over, the syndicate may have sold out all its bonds and its foreign members have been put in a position where they can pay off all the drafts they set afloat originally in order to raise the money.

Very often, however, it will happen that on account of one reason or another, sixty days pass or ninety days pass without the syndicate having been able to dispose of its bonds. In that case the long bills drawn on the foreign bankers have to be "renewed"--that being a process for which ample provision has, of course, been made. In a succeeding chapter, full description of how long bills of exchange coming due are renewed will be made. Just here it is only necessary to say that most or all of the money necessary to pay off the maturing bills is raised by selling another batch of "sixties" or "nineties," an operation which throws the maturity two or three months further ahead.

From this outline of the way foreign participation in American bond issues is financed, it can be seen that every time a big issue of bonds of a railroad or industrial in which European investors are actively interested, is brought out, it means a large supply of foreign exchange created and suddenly thrown on the exchange market for sale. Not any more suddenly or publicly than the bankers concerned can help, but still necessarily so to a great degree, because big bond issues can only be made with the full knowledge and cooperation of a large part of the public. Bankers who know in advance of large issues likely to be made and in which they know they will be asked to participate, often sell "futures" covering the exchange they foresee their participation will bring into existence, but as a general rule it may be set down that heavy issues, involving the sale abroad of large amounts of bonds, are a most depressing factor on the foreign exchange market. Especially so, as the participants who have agreed to turn over the money to the railroad, must sell bills to raise it, even if the horde of speculators and "trailers" who are always on the lookout for such opportunities, make every effort to sell the market out from under their feet.

3. Uneasiness with regard to the stability of the financial situation at some point abroad where American bankers usually carry large balances is another circumstance which often depresses the exchange market sharply. "Trouble in the Balkans" and "trouble over the Moroccan situation" are two bugbears which have for years back furnished the keynote for many swoops downward in the exchange market, and for years after this book is published will probably continue to do so. Money on deposit at a point several thousand miles away is naturally very sensitive, and the least suspicion of financial trouble is sufficient to cause its withdrawal. Withdrawal of bankers' balances from a foreign city means offerings of exchange drawn on that point with resultant decline in rates.

In the everyday life of the exchange market, political developments of an unfavorable character and war rumors are about the most frequent and potent influences toward the condition of uneasiness above referred to. Few war rumors ever come to anything, but there are times when they circulate with astonishing frequency and persistence and cause decided uneasiness concerning financial conditions at important points. At such times bankers having money on deposit at those points are apt to become influenced by the drift of sentiment and to draw down their balances. Here, again, operators in exchange, keenly on the alert for such chances, will very likely begin to sell the exchange market short and often succeed in breaking it to a degree entirely unwarranted by the known facts.

4. But of all the sure depressing influences on exchange, none is more sure than a rise in the money market. More gradual usually than a decline caused by such an influence as the sale of American bonds abroad, the influence of a rising level of money rates is nevertheless far more certain.

The theory of this "counter" movement in money rates and exchange is simply that when money rates rise, say at a point like New York, American bankers find it profitable to draw in their deposits from all over Europe for the purpose of using the money in New York. Such a process means a wholesale drawing of bills of exchange on all the leading European cities, with consequent offering of the bills and price-depression in the leading American exchange markets.

The number of banks scattered all over the United States which keep running deposit accounts in the leading European cities has become surprisingly great during the past ten years, and a movement to bring home this capital has to go only a little way before it reaches very large proportions. That is exactly what happens when money rates at a point like New York become decidedly more attractive than they are over on the other side. Arrangements with foreign correspondents usually call for a minimum balance of considerable size, which must be left intact, but under ordinary circumstances there is considerable leeway, and when the better opportunity for loaning presents itself here, drafts on balances abroad, in large aggregate amount, are apt to be drawn and sold in this market. Especially is this the case when the cause of the higher money level appears to be deep-rooted and the outlook is for a continuance of the condition for some time to come.

5. Lastly, as a depressing factor, there is to be considered the condition which arises when money at some important foreign center, such as London or Paris, begins to ease decidedly. Large receipts of gold from the mines, a bettering political outlook--these or many other causes may bring it about that money in London, for instance, after a period of high rates, may ease off faster than in Berlin or Hamburg. As a result, American bankers having large balances in London and finding it difficult to employ them profitably there, any longer, either withdraw them entirely or have the money transferred to some other point. In either case the operation will result in depressing the rate of exchange on London, for the American banker will either draw on London himself or, if he wants to transfer the money to Berlin or Hamburg, will instruct the German bankers by cable to draw for his account on London. In whatever way it is accomplished, the withdrawal of capital from any

banking point tends to lower the rate of foreign exchange on that point.

These are the main influences bearing on the fluctuation of exchange. Needless to say they are not exerted all one way, or one at a time, as set forth. The international money markets are a most decidedly complex proposition, and there is literally never a time when several influences tending to put rates up are not conflicting with several influences tending to put rates down. The actual movement of the rate represents the relative strength of the two sets of influences. To be able to "size up" the influences present and to gauge what movement of rates they will result in, is an operation requiring, first, knowledge, then judgment. The former qualification can perhaps be derived, in small degree, from study of the foregoing pages. The latter is a matter of mental calibre and experience.

CHAPTER IV

THE VARIOUS KINDS OF EXCHANGE

Before taking up the question of the activities of the foreign exchange department and the question of how bankers make money dealing in exchange, it may be well to fix in mind clearly what the various forms of foreign exchange are. Following is a description of the most important classes of bills bought and sold in the New York market:

1. Commercial Long Bills

Drafts drawn by shippers of merchandise upon buyers abroad, or upon the banking representatives of the buyers abroad, at thirty days' sight or more. The drafts may be accompanied by shipping documents or may be "clean." The former kind of bill making up the greater part of the whole amount of foreign exchange dealt in in the New York market, will be described first.

Suppose a cotton dealer in Memphis to have sold one hundred bales of cotton to a spinner in Liverpool, the arrangement being that the English buyer is to be drawn on at sixty days' sight. The first thing the Memphis merchant does is to ship the cotton on its way to Liverpool, receiving from the railroad company a receipt known as a "bill of lading." At the same time he arranges for the insurance of the cotton, receiving from the insurance company a little certificate stating that the insurance has been effected.

The next step is for the Memphis shipper to draw the draft on the Liverpool buyer--or upon some bank abroad designated by the buyer. This draft is drawn in pounds sterling for the equivalent of the dollar value of the cotton and made payable sixty days after the party abroad on whom it is drawn has seen it and written "accepted" across its face. This draft, the bill of lading received from the shipping company, and the insurance certificate received from the insurance company are then pinned together and constitute a complete "commercial long bill with documents attached."

Other less important documents go with such a bill. Sometimes invoices showing the weight and price of the cotton go along with it and sometimes there is also attached a "hypothecation slip" which formally turns over the right to the goods to the Memphis or New York banker who buys the draft and accompanying documents from the Memphis cotton shipper. Sometimes, too, insurance is effected by the buyer abroad, in which case there may be no insurance certificate. But in the main, one of these "documentary" commercial bills consists of the draft itself, the bill of lading, and an insurance certificate.

Having pinned the document and the draft together, the Memphis cotton shipper is in possession of an instrument which he can dispose of for dollars. This he does either by selling it to his bank in Memphis or by sending it to New York, in order that it may be sold there in the exchange market at the current rate of exchange. Say, the bill of exchange is drawn on London at sixty days' sight, for ?,000. The buying price for such a draft will be, perhaps, 4.84. The Memphis shipper gets his check for $4,840, and is out of the transaction. The bill has passed into a banker's hands, who will send it abroad--deposit it in some foreign bank where he keeps a balance.

As to the rate of 4.84 received by the shipper, it is to be noted that had the bill been drawn at less than sixty days' sight, he would have received more dollars for it, while if it had been drawn at more than sixty days' sight, he would have received less for it. The longer the banker who takes the draft off the shipper's hands has to wait until he can get his money back on it, the lower, naturally, the rate of exchange he is willing to pay. On the same day that demand drafts are selling at 4.87, sixty-day drafts may be selling at 4.84 and ninety-day drafts at 4.83.

Assume, in this particular case, that the draft has been taken off the shipper's hands by some foreign exchange banker in New York. By the very first steamer the latter will forward it to his banking correspondent abroad, with instructions to present it at once to the parties on whom it is drawn, in order that they may mark it "accepted--payable such-and-such-a-date." After that the bill is a double obligation of the drawer and the drawee, and may be discounted in the open market, for cash.

Just here it is necessary to digress and state that documentary commercial bills are of two kinds--"acceptance" bills and "payment" bills. In the case of the first-named, the documents are delivered to the party on whom the bill is drawn as soon as he "accepts" the bill, which puts him in a position to get possession of the merchandise at once. In the case of a "payment" bill, the credit of the man on whom it is drawn is not good enough to entitle him to such a privilege, and the only way he can get actual possession of the goods is to actually pay the draft under a rebate-of-interest arrangement. All bills drawn on banks are naturally "acceptance" bills; and being discountable and thus immediately convertible into cash abroad, command a better rate of exchange in the New York market than "payment" bills, which may be allowed to run all the way to maturity before a single pound sterling is paid on them.

Except in the case of the shipment of perishable merchandise--grain shipped in bulk, for instance. In that case the buyer on the other side cannot afford to let the draft run, because the merchandise would spoil. He is simply forced to pay it under rebate, in order to get possession of the grain. And the rebate being always less than the discount rate, less pounds sterling come off the face of the bill in the process of rebating than of discounting. For which reason sixty-day bills drawn against shipments of grain--documents deliverable only on payment under rebate--command a better rate of exchange even than the very best of cotton "acceptance" bills drawn on banks.

2. Clean Bills

Where the drafts of the merchants of one country drawn upon the merchants or bankers of another are unaccompanied by shipping documents they are said to be "clean." Bills of this kind may originate from the transfer of capital from one country to another or may represent drawings against shipments of merchandise previously made. It is not unusual, indeed, where the relationship between some foreign merchant and some American merchant is very close, for the one to ship merchandise to the other without drawing drafts against the shipment until some little time afterward. It might happen, for instance, that a cotton manufacturing firm in France wanted to import a lot of raw cotton from the United States, but did not want to be drawn upon at the time. Under such circumstances the American house might ship the goods and send over the documents to the buyer, postponing its drawing for some time. Eventually, of course, the American house would reimburse itself by drawing, but the documents having gone forward long before, the drafts would be what is known as "clean."

Later on, in the chapter on the actual money-making operations of the foreign department, the risk in buying various kinds of bills will be fully explained, but in passing it may be mentioned that "clean" bills are of such a nature that bankers will touch them only when drawn by the very best houses. With a documentary bill, the banker holds the bill of lading, and if there is any trouble about the acceptance or payment of a draft, can simply seize the goods and sell them. But in the case of a "clean" bill, he has absolutely no security. The standing of the maker of the bill and what he knows about the maker's right to draw the bill is all he has to go by in determining whether to buy it or not.

3. Documentary Commercial Bills Drawn at Short Sight

A comparatively small part of our exports are sold on a basis where the draft drawn is at less than thirty days' sight, but there are a good many small bills of this kind continually coming into the market. Drafts drawn against manufactured articles and against such products as cheese, butter, dried fruits, etc., are apt to be drawn for, with shipping documents attached, at anywhere from three to thirty days' sight, but there is no rule about it. Where the "usance"--the time the bill has to run--is only a few days, documents are apt to be deliverable only on payment of the bills.

4. Drafts Drawn Against Securities

Exchange of this kind is naturally of the highest class, the stocks or bonds against which it is drawn being almost always attached to the bill of exchange. In the case of syndicate participations by large houses, the bonds may be shipped abroad privately and exchange against them drawn and sold independently, in which case, of course, no security is attached, but as a rule the bonds or stocks go with the draft. A, in New York, executes an order to buy for B in London, one hundred Union Pacific preferred shares on the New York Stock Exchange. The stock comes into A's office, and he pays for it with the proceeds of a sterling draft he draws on B. The stock itself he attaches to this sterling draft. Whoever buys the draft of him gets the stock with it and keeps possession of it till the draft is presented and paid in London.

5. Bankers' Checks or Demand Drafts on Their Correspondents Abroad

Bankers who do a foreign exchange business, keeping large balances in several European centers, are continually drawing and selling their demand drafts--"checks," they are called, or "demand"--upon these foreign balances.

Such checks are always to be had in great volume in the exchange market, the banker's business being to draw and sell exchange, and his degree of willingness being merely a matter of rate. There come times, of course, when bankers have every reason to leave their foreign balances undisturbed, but even at such times the bid of a high enough rate will usually bring about the drawing of bills.

6. Bankers' Long Drafts

In describing the nature of bankers' drawings of long bills, great care must be taken to differentiate between the different kinds of long bills being bought and sold in the exchange market. A finance bill looks exactly the same as a long bill drawn by a banker for a commercial customer who wants to anticipate the payment abroad for an incoming shipment of wool or shellac, but the nature and origin of the two bills are radically different. The three main kinds of bankers' long bills will thus be taken up in the following order:

A. Bills Drawn in the Regular Course of Business

Such is the nature of foreign exchange business that bankers engaged in it are continually drawing their sixty and ninety days' sight bills in response to their own and their customers' needs. One example which might be cited is that of the importer who has a payment to make on the other side, sixty days from now, but who, having the money on hand, wants to make it at once. Under some circumstances such an importer might remit a demand draft on the basis of receiving a rebate of interest for the unexpired sixty days, but more likely he would go to a banker and buy from him a sixty days' sight draft for the exact amount of pounds he owed. The cost of such a draft--which would mature at the time the debt became due--would be less than the cost of a demand draft, the importer getting his rebate of interest out of the cheaper price he pays for the pounds he needs. Prepayments of this sort are responsible every day for very large drawings of bankers' long bills.

B. Long Bills Issued in the Operation of Lending Foreign Money

Bills of this kind represent by far the greater proportion of bankers' long bills sold in the exchange market. European bankers keep an enormous amount of floating capital loaned out in this market, in the making and renewing of which loans long bills are created as follows:

A banker on the other side decides to loan out, say, ?00,000 in the New York market. Arrangements having been made, he cables his New York representative to draw ninety days' sight drafts on him for ?00,000, the proceeds of which drafts are then loaned out for account of the foreign house. The matter of collateral, risk of exchange and, indeed, all the other detail, will be fully described in the succeeding chapters on how bankers make money out of exchange. For the time being it is merely necessary to note that every time a loan of foreign capital is made here--and there are days when millions of pounds are so loaned out--bankers' long bills for the full amount of the loans are created and find their way into the exchange market.

C. Bankers' Long Bills Drawn for the Purpose of Raising Money

Finance bills constitute the third kind of bankers' long exchange. In this case, again, detailed discussion must be put off until the chapter on foreign-exchange-bankers' operations, but the fact that bills of this kind constitute so important a part of the bankers' long bills to be had in the market, necessitates their classification in this place. Every time a banker here starts to use his credit abroad for the purpose of raising money--and there are times when the privilege is pretty freely availed of--he does it by drawing sixty or ninety days' sight drafts on his correspondents abroad. Finance bills, it may be said without question, are one of the most interesting forms of foreign exchange banking--at the same time one of the most useful and one of the most abused of privileges coming to the domestic banker by reason of his having strong banking connections abroad.

CHAPTER V

THE FOREIGN EXCHANGE MARKET

The foreign exchange market is in every sense "open"--anyone with bills to buy or sell and whose credit is all right can enter it and do business on a par with anyone else. There is no place where the trading is done, no membership, license or anything of the kind. The "market," in fact, exists in name only; it is really constituted of a number of banks, dealers and brokers, with offices in the same section of the city, and who do business indiscriminately among themselves--sometimes personally, sometimes by telephone, by messenger, or by the aid of the continuously circulating exchange brokers.

The system is about as follows: The larger banks and banking houses have a foreign exchange manager, or partner, taking care of that part of the business, whose office is usually so situated as to make him accessible to the brokers who come in from the outside, and whose telephoning and wiring facilities are very complete. These larger houses have no brokers or "outside" men in their employ. The manager knows very well that plenty of chance to do business, buying or selling, will be brought in to him by the brokers and that his wires keep him constantly in touch with his fellow bankers.

Next come the big dealers in exchange, some of whom do a regular exchange business of their own, the same as the bankers, but who also have men out on the street "trading" between large buyers and sellers of bills. Such houses are necessarily closely in touch with banks, bankers, exporters, and importers all over the country, and have always large orders on hand to buy and sell exchange. Some of the bills they handle they buy and use for the conduct of their own business with banks abroad, but the more important part of what they do is to deal in foreign exchange among the banks. They are known as always having on hand for sale large lines of commercial and bankers' bills, while on the other hand they are always ready to buy, at the right price.

After this class of houses come the regular brokers--the independent and unattached individuals who spend their time trying to bring buyer and seller together, and make a commission out of doing it. In a market like New York the number of exchange brokers is very large. Like bond-brokerage, the business requires little in the way of office facilities or capital, and is attractive to a good many persons who are willing to accept the small income to be made out of it in return for being in a business where they are independent.

Foreign exchange brokerage, like all other employment of the middleman, is not what it used to be. Before the business became overcrowded as it is now, exchange brokers made their quarter-cent in the pound commission, and could depend on a respectable income. But nowadays brokers swarm among the foreign exchange bankers and dealers, doing business on any commission they can get, which is not infrequently as little as 1/128 of one per cent., say, $1.50, for buying or selling francs 100,000. In handling sterling, the broker is lucky if he makes his five points (5/100 of a cent per pound), which means that for turning over ?0,000 he would be rewarded with the sum of $5. Under such conditions it is not difficult to see how hard it is to make any money to speak of out of foreign exchange brokerage.

The dealers, of course, fare much better. Handling commercial bills where the question of credit affects the price, they have a chance to make more of a profit, and buying and selling bills for their own account they naturally are entitled to make more than the man without capital, who simply tries to get in between the buyer and the seller. Dealing in exchange, especially for out-of-town clients, is a highly profitable business, but one which takes time, brains, experience and money to build up. Dealers representing large out-of-town sellers of exchange are very much in the position of the New York agents of manufacturing companies who sell goods on commission.

There being no regular market in which foreign exchange rates are made, it follows that the establishment of rates each morning and during the course of each day will be according to the supply and demand for bills. On any given morning by ten o'clock the bankers will all have received their cables quoting money and exchange rates in the foreign centers, and will all have pretty well made up their minds as to what the rate for demand bills on London ought to be. A banker, for instance, has ?0,000 he wants to sell as early in the morning as possible, and from his foreign cables figures that 4.86 is about the right price. He offers it at that, but learns that another banker is offering exchange at 4.8595. He offers his own at that price, and somebody comes along, taking both lots and bidding 4.86 for ?0,000 more. Somebody else bids 4.86 for other large lots, refusing, however, to pay 4.8605. The market is established at that point.

For the time being. A cable message from abroad may induce some banker to bid 4.8605 or 4.8610, or it may cause him to throw on the market such an amount of exchange as may break the price down to 4.85-3/4. Rates are constantly changing, and changing at times almost from minute to minute. Yet so complete is the system of telephones and brokers that any exchange manager can tell just about what is taking place in any other part of the market. Not infrequently, of course, sales are made simultaneously at slightly different rates, but, as a rule, if a trade is made at 4.86 on Cedar Street, 4.86 will be the rate on Exchange Place. It is remarkable how closely each manager keeps in touch with what is going on in every part of the market. And the great number of brokers continually circulating around and trying to "get in between" for five points is in itself a powerful influence toward keeping rates exactly the same in all parts of the market at once.

"Posted rates" mean little with regard to current conditions, being simply the bankers' public notice of the rate at which he will sell bills for trifling amounts. Exchange bankers dislike to draw small drafts and usually can be induced to do so only by the offer of a much higher rate than that current for a large amount. A banker might offer to sell you ?0,000 at 4.87, but if you said you wanted only ?0, he would be likely to point to his posted rate and charge you 4.88. Considering that in transactions based on the best bills the banker only figures on making from $10 to $20 profit on each ?0,000, it may readily be seen why he is not anxious to sell a ?0 draft.

As to the actual fluctuation of exchange, while it is true that rates at times rise and fall with all the violence so often displayed in the security markets, most of the time they move within a comparatively narrow range. On an ordinary business day, for instance, the change is not apt to run over fifteen points (15/100 of a cent per pound). In the morning, demand sterling may be at, say, 4.86; at noon a moderate demand for bills may carry the rate, first, to 4.8605, then to 4.8610; and finally, perhaps, to 4.8615. On fairly large offerings of bills the market might then recede to, say, 4.8605, ending the day five points up. And that would be an ordinary day--by no means the kind of a day the exchange market always sees, but a day corresponding to a stock market session in which the market leaders rise or fall a point or so.

There are times, of course, when very different conditions prevail. An unexpected rise in the bank rate in London, the announcement of a big loan or any one of many different happenings, are apt to cause a reduction in the exchange market and a bewildering movement of rates up and down. At such times a rise or fall of fifty points in sterling within half an hour is not at all out of the ordinary, while in times of panic, or when great crises impend, the fluctuations will be three or four times as great. During the latter part of October, 1907, and in November, the exchange market fluctuated with greater violence than, perhaps, at any other time since the gold standard was firmly established. Thrown completely out of gear by the premium of 3-1/2 per cent. a day for currency during the panic time, the exchange markets for some time would rise and fall several cents in the pound on the same day. Completely baffled by this erratic movement, many bankers temporarily withdrew entirely from the market.

As to the relative importance of the different kinds of exchange, sterling, of course, occupies the most prominent position. What proportion of the total of exchange dealt in in the New York market consists of sterling it is impossible to determine, but that it is as great as the volume of all the other kinds of exchange put together can safely be said. Many big dealers, indeed, make a specialty of sterling, and if they handle any other bills at all, do so only on a very small scale. As to whether francs or marks come next in volume, there is a difference of opinion. With Germany our direct financial transactions are probably considerably larger than with France, but the position of Paris as a banking centre makes the French capital figure prominently in many operations where the French market is not directly concerned. Despite the fact that sterling easily predominates, the volume of franc and mark bills, too, is enormous. Drafts on Paris for from three to five million francs and on Berlin for as many marks are not at all infrequently traded in in the exchange market, and at times bills for very much larger amounts have been drawn and offered for sale.

Bills drawn in other kinds of currency--guilders on Holland, for instance, form an important part of the foreign exchange dealt in in a market like New York, but are subservient in their rate fluctuations to the movement of sterling, marks, and francs. The latter are, indeed, the three great classes of exchange, and are the basis of at least nine-tenths of all foreign exchange operations.

In the following chapter will be taken up the various forms of activity of the foreign exchange department. No attempt is made to state out of which kind of business bankers make most money, but before looking into the more detailed description of how exchange business is conducted, it may be well to fix in mind the fact that it is out of the "straight" forms of foreign exchange business that the most profit is made. Highly complicated operations are indulged in by some managers with more theoretical than practical sense, and money is at times made out of them, but on the whole the real money is made out of the kinds of business about to be described. To the author's certain knowledge, the exchange business of one of the largest houses in New York was for years thus limited to what might be called "straight" operations. While the profits might at times have been materially increased by the introduction of a little more of a speculative element into the business, the house made money on a large scale and avoided the losses inevitable where business is conducted along speculative lines.

CHAPTER VI

HOW MONEY IS MADE IN FOREIGN EXCHANGE. THE OPERATIONS OF THE FOREIGN DEPARTMENT

Complete description of the various forms of activity of the foreign exchange department of an important firm would fill a large volume, but there are certain stock operations in foreign exchange which are the basis of most of the transactions carried out and the understanding of which ought to go a long way toward making clear what the nature of the foreign exchange department's business really is.

1. Selling "Demand" Against "Demand"

The first and most elementary form of activity is, of course, the buying of demand bills at a certain price and the selling of the banker's own demand drafts against them at a higher price. A banker finds, for instance, that he can buy John Smith & Co.'s sight draft for ?,000, on London, at the rate of 4.86, and that he can sell his own draft for ?,000 on his London banking correspondent at 4.87. All he has to do, therefore, is to buy John Smith's draft for $4,860, send it to London for credit of his account there, and then draw his own draft for ?,000 on the newly created balance, selling it for $4,870. It cost him $4,860 to buy the commercial draft, and he has sold his own draft against it for $4,870. His gross profit on the transaction, therefore, is $10.

As may be imagined, not very much money is made in transactions exactly of this kind--the one cited is taken only because it illustrates the principle. For whether the banker sends over in every mail a bewildering assortment of every conceivable form of foreign exchange to be credited to his account abroad, or whether he confines himself to remittances of the simplest kinds of bills, the idea remains exactly the same--he is depositing money to the credit of his account in order that he may have a balance on which he can draw. That is, indeed, the sum and substance of the exchange business of the foreign department of most banking houses--the maintaining of deposit accounts in banks at foreign centers on which deposit account the bank here is in a position to draw according to the wants and needs of its customers.

To analyze the underlying transaction a little more closely, it is evident that the banker, in order to make a profit, must be able to buy the commercial bill at a lower rate of exchange than he can realize on his own draft. Which suggests at once that the extent of the banker's profit is dependent largely upon the amount of risk he is willing to take. For the rate on commercial bills is purely a matter of the drawer's credit. The best documentary commercial exchange, drawn at sight on banks abroad or houses of the highest standing will command a rate of exchange in the open market only a little less than the banker's own draft. From which point the rate realizable on commercial bills tapers off with the credit of the house in question, some bills regularly selling a cent or a cent and a half per pound sterling below the best bills of their class.

Without the introduction, therefore, of the element of speculation, except as to the soundness of the bills' makers, it is possible for bankers to make widely varying profits out of the same kind of business. Everything depends upon the amount of risk the banker is willing to take. The exchange market is a merciless critic of credit, and if a commercial firm's bills always sell at low rates, the presumption is strongly against its financial strength. Cases very frequently occur, however, where the exchange market misjudges the goodness of a bill, placing too low a valuation upon it. In that case the banker who, individually, knows that the house in question is all right, can make considerable sums of money buying its bills at the low-going rates and selling his own exchange against them. This, evidently, is purely a matter of the exchange manager's judgment. With comparatively little risk there are banking houses which are making a full cent a pound out of a good part of the commercial exchange they handle.

2. Selling Cables Against Demand Exchange

No description of a cable transfer having been given in the preceding description of different kinds of exchange, it may be explained briefly that a "cable," so-called, differs from a sight draft only in that the banker abroad who is to pay out the money is advised to do so by means of a telegraphic message instead of by a bit of paper instructing him to "pay to the order of so and so." A, in New York, wants to transfer money to B, in London. He goes to his banker in New York and deposits the amount, in dollars, with him, requesting that he (the New York banker) instruct his correspondent in London, by cable, to pay to B the equivalent in pounds. The transfer is immediate, the cable being sent as soon as the American banker receives the money on this end.

To be able to instruct its correspondent in London by cable to pay out large sums at any given time, a bank here must necessarily carry a substantial credit balance abroad. It would be possible, of course, for a banker to instruct his London agent by cable to pay out a sum of money, at the same time cabling him the money to pay out, but this operation of selling cables against cables is not much indulged in--there is too little chance of profit in it. Under special circumstances, however, it can be seen that a house anxious to sell a large cable and not having the balance abroad to do it, might easily provide its correspondent abroad with the funds by going out and buying a cable itself.

But under ordinary circumstances foreign exchange dealers who engage in the business of selling cables carry adequate balances on the other side, balances which they keep replenishing by continuous remittances of demand exchange. Which in itself constitutes an important form of foreign exchange activity and an operation out of which many large houses make a good deal of money.

All the parties involved being bankers there is little risk in business of this kind; but, on the other hand, the margin of profit is small, and in order to make any money out of it, it is necessary that very large amounts of money be turned over. The average profit, for instance, realized in the New York exchange market from straight sales of cables against remittances of checks is fifteen points (15/100 of a cent per pound sterling). That means that on every

?0,000, the gross profit would be $15.00. A daily turnover of ?0,000, therefore, would result in a gross profit of $75 a day.

It may seem strange that bankers should be willing to turn over so large an amount of money for so small a profit, even where the risk has been reduced to a minimum, but that is the case. Very often cables are sold against balances which have been accumulated by remittance of all sorts of bills other than demand, but there are several large American institutions whose foreign exchange business consists principally of the regulation selling of cables against remittances of demand bills. By reason of their large deposits they are in a position to carry full balances abroad, while in the course of their regular business a good deal of sight exchange of high class comes across their counters. All the necessary elements for doing the business being there, it only remains for such an institution to employ a man capable of directing the actual transactions. The risk is trifling, the advertisement is world-wide, the accommodation of customers is being attended to, and there is considerable actual money profit to be made. The business in many respects is thus highly desirable.

3. Selling "Demand" Bills Against Remittances of Long Bills

If there is a stock operation in the conduct of a foreign exchange business it is the selling by bankers of their demand bills of exchange against remittances of commercial and bankers' long paper. Bills of the latter class, as has been pointed out, make up the bulk of foreign exchange traded in, and its disposal naturally is the most important phase of foreign exchange business. For after all, all cabling, arbitraging in exchange, drawing of finance bills, etc., is only incidental. What the foreign exchange business really is grounded on is the existence of commercial bills called into existence by exports of merchandise.

There are houses doing an extensive exchange business who never buy commercial long bills, but the operations they carry on are made possible only by the fact that most other houses do. A foreign exchange department which does not handle this kind of exchange is necessarily on the "outside" of the real business--is like a bond broker who does not carry bonds with his own money but merely trades in and out on other people's operations.

Buying and remitting commercial long bills is, however, no pastime for an inexperienced man. Entirely aside from the question of rate, and profit on the exchange end of the transaction, there must be taken into consideration the matter of the credit of the drawer and the drawee, the salability of the merchandise specified in the bill of lading, and a number of other important points. This question of credit, underlying to so great a degree the whole business of buying commercial long paper, will be considered first.

The completely equipped exchange department has at its disposal all the machinery necessary for investigating expeditiously the standing and financial strength of any firm whose bills are likely to be offered in the exchange market. Such facilities are afforded by subscription to the two leading mercantile agencies, but in addition to this, the experienced exchange manager has at his command private sources of information which can be applied to practically every firm engaged in the export business. The larger banks, of course, all have a regular credit man, one of whose chief duties nowadays is to assist in the handling of the bank's foreign exchange business. So perfect does the organization become after a few years of the actual transaction of a foreign exchange business that the standing of practically any bill taken by a broker into a bank, for sale, can be passed upon instantly. New firms come into existence, of course, and have to be fully investigated, but the experienced manager of a foreign department can tell almost offhand whether he wants a bill of any given name or not.

Where documents accompany the draft and the merchandise is formally hypothecated to the buyer of the draft, it might not be thought that the standing of the drawer would be of such great importance. Possession of the merchandise, it is true, gives the banker a certain form of security in case acceptance of the bill is refused by the parties on whom it is drawn or in case they refuse to pay it when it comes due, but the disposal of such collateral is a burdensome and often expensive operation. The banker in New York who buys a sixty-day draft drawn against a shipment of butter is presumably not an expert on the butter market and if he should be forced to sell the butter, might not be able to do so to the fullest possible advantage. Employment of an expert agent is an expensive operation, and, moreover, there is always the danger of legal complication arising out of the banker's having sold the collateral. It is desirable in every way that if there is to be any trouble about the acceptance or payment of a draft, the banker should keep himself out of it.

A concrete illustration of the dangers attendant upon the purchase of commercial long bills from irresponsible parties is to be found in what happened a few years ago to a prominent exchange house in New York. This house had been buying the bills of a certain firm for some little time, and everything had gone well. But one day acceptance of a bill for ?,000 was refused by the party abroad, and the news cabled that the bill of lading was a forgery and that no such shipment had ever been made. Wiring hurriedly to the inland city in which was located the firm which drew the bill, the New York bank received the reply that both partners had decamped. What had happened was that, about to break up, the "firm" had drawn and sold several large bills of exchange, with forged documents attached, received their money for them, and then disappeared. Neither of them was ever apprehended, and the various bankers who had taken the exchange lost the money they had paid for it. Forgery of the bill of lading in this case had been a comparatively easy matter, the shipment purporting to have been made from an obscure little cotton town in the South, the signature of whose railroad agent was not at all known.

This forgery is only one example of the trickery possible and the extreme care which is necessary in the purchase of bills of this kind. And not only must the standing of the drawer be taken into consideration, but the standing of the drawee is a matter of almost equal importance--after the "acceptance" of the bill, the parties accepting it being equally liable with its maker. The nature of the merchandise, furthermore, and its marketability are further considerations of great importance. Cotton, it will readily appear, is an entirely different sort of collateral from clocks, or some specialty in which the market may vary widely. The banker who holds a bill of lading for cotton shipped to Liverpool can at any moment tell exactly what he can realize on it. In the case of many kinds of articles, however, the invoice value may differ widely from the realizable value, and if the banker should ever be forced to sell the merchandise, he might have to do so at a big loss.

Returning to the actual operation of selling bankers' demand against remittances of long bills, it appears that the successive steps in an actual transaction are about as follows:

The banker in New York having ascertained by cable the rate at which bills "to arrive" in London by a certain steamer will be discounted, buys the bills here and sends them over, with instructions that they be immediately discounted and the proceeds placed to his credit. On this resulting balance he will at once draw his demand draft and sell it in the open market. If, from selling this demand draft, he can realize more dollars than it cost him in dollars to put the balance over there, he has made a gross profit of the difference.

To illustrate more specifically: A banker has bought, say, a ?,000 ninety days' sight prime draft, on London, documents deliverable on acceptance. This he has remitted to his foreign correspondent, and his foreign correspondent has had it stamped with the required "bill-stamp," has had it discounted, and after having taken his commission out of the proceeds, has had them placed to the credit of the American bank. In all this process the bill has lost weight. It arrived in London as ?,000, but after commissions, bill-stamps and ninety-three days' discount have been taken out of it, the amount is reduced well below ?,000. The net proceeds going to make up the balance on which the American banker can draw his draft are, perhaps, not over ?90. He paid so-and-so many dollars for the ?,000 ninety-day bill, originally. If he can realize that many dollars by selling a demand draft for ?90 he is even on the transaction.

No attempt will be made in this little book to present the tables by which foreign exchange bankers figure out profit possibilities in operations of this kind. The terms obtainable from foreign correspondents vary so widely according to the standing and credit of the house on this side and are governed by so many different influences that a manager must work out each transaction he enters according to the conditions by which he, particularly, and his operations are governed. Such calculations, moreover, are all built up along the general line of the scheme presented below:

Assume that the rate for demand bills is 4.85, that discount in London is 3-1/2 per cent, and that the amount of the long bill remitted for discount and credit of proceeds is ?00.

The various expenses are as follows:

Commission charged by the banker in London 1/40 per cent. $0.12

Discount, 93 days (3 days of grace) at 3-1/2 per cent. 4.38

English Government bill stamp 1/20 per cent. 0.24 ------ $4.74

Total charges on the ninety days' sight ?00 bill amount to $4.74. On one pound, therefore, the charge would be $.0474. From which it is evident that each pound of a ninety-day bill, under the conditions given, is worth $.0474 (=4.74 cents) less than each pound in a bankers' demand bill. From which it is evident that if such a demand bill were sold at 4.85 against a ninety-day bill bought at 4.8026 (found by subtracting 4.74 cents from 485 cents) the remitting banker would come out even in the transaction.

The foregoing has been introduced at the risk of confusing the lay reader, on the idea that all the various calculations regarding the drawing of "demand" against the remitting of long bills are founded on the same general principle, and that where it is desired to go more deeply into the matter the correct conditions can be substituted. Discount, of course, varies from day to day, "payment" bills do not go through the discount market at all, but are "rebated," the commissions charged different bankers and by different bankers vary widely. Under the circumstances the value of presenting a lot of hard-and-fast calculations worked out under any given set of conditions is extremely doubtful.

As to the profit on business of this kind it can be said that the average, where the best bills are used, runs not much over twenty points (one-fifth of a cent per pound sterling). From that, of course, profits actually made run up as high as one cent or even two cents per pound, according to the amount of risk involved. The buying of cheap bills is, however, a most precarious operation. One single mistake, and the whole profit of months may be completely wiped out. The proposition is a good deal like lending money on insecure collateral, or like lending to doubtful firms. There are banking houses which do it, have been doing it for years, and by reason of an intuitive feeling when there is trouble ahead have been able to avoid heavy losses. Such business, however, can hardly be called high-class banking practice.

4. The Operation of Making Foreign Loans

In its influence upon the other markets, there is perhaps no more important phase of foreign exchange than the making of foreign loans in the American market. How great is the amount of foreign capital continually loaned out in this country has been several times suggested in previous pages. The mechanics of these foreign loaning operations, the way in which the money is transferred to this side, etc., will now be taken up.

To begin at the very beginning, consider how favorable a field is the American market for the employment of Europe's spare banking capital. Almost invariably loaning rates in New York are higher than they are in London or Paris. This is due, perhaps, to the fact that industry here runs on at a much faster pace than in England or France, or it may be due to the fact that we are a newer country, that there is no such accumulated fund of capital here as there is abroad. Such a hypothesis for our own higher interest rates would seem to be supported by the fact that in Germany, too, interest is consistently on a higher level than in London or Paris, Germany, like ourselves, being a vigorous industrial nation without any very great accumulated fund of capital saved by the people. But whatever the reason, the fact remains that in New York money rates are generally on so much more attractive a basis than they are abroad that there is practically never a time when there are not hundreds of millions of dollars of English and French money loaned out in this market.

To go back no further than the present decade, it will be recalled how great a part foreign floating capital played in financing the ill-starred speculation here which culminated in the panic of May 9, 1901. Europe in the end of 1900 had gone mad over our industrial combinations and had shovelled her millions into this market for the use of our promoters. What use was made of the money is well known. The instance is mentioned here, with others which follow, only to show that all through the past ten years London has at various times opened her reservoirs of capital and literally poured money into the American market.

Even the experience of 1901 did not daunt the foreign lenders, and in 1902 fresh amounts of foreign capital, this time mostly German, were secured by our speculators to push along the famous "Gates boom." That time, however, the lenders' experience seemed to discourage them, and until 1906 there was not a great deal of foreign money, relatively speaking, loaned out here. In the summer of that year, chiefly through Mr. Harriman's efforts, English and French capital began to come largely into the New York market--made possible, indeed, the "Harriman Market of 1906." This was the money the terror-stricken withdrawal of which during most of 1907 made the panic as bad as it was. After the panic, most of what was left was withdrawn by foreign lenders, so that in the middle of 1908 the market here was as bare of foreign money as it has been in years. Returning American prosperity, however, combined with complete stagnation abroad, set up another hitherward movement of foreign capital which, during the spring and summer of 1909, attained amazing proportions. By the end of the summer, indeed, more foreign capital was employed in the American market than ever before in the country's financial history.

To take up the actual operation of loaning foreign money in the American market, suppose conditions to be such that an English bank's managers have made up their minds to loan out ?00,000 in New York--not on joint account with the American correspondent, as is often done, but entirely independently. Included in the arrangements for the transaction will be a stipulation as to whether the foreign bank loaning the money wants to loan it on the basis of receiving a commission and letting the borrower take the risk of how demand exchange may fluctuate during the life of the loan, or whether the lender prefers to lend at a fixed rate of interest, say six per cent., and himself accept the risk of exchange.

What the foregoing means will perhaps become more clear if it is realized that in the first case the American agent of the foreign lender draws a ninety days' sight sterling bill for, say, ?00,000 on the lender, and hands the actual bill over to the parties here who want the money. Upon the latter falls the task of selling the bill, and, ninety days later, when the time of repayment comes, the duty of returning a demand bill for ?00,000, plus the stipulated commission. In the second kind of a loan the borrower has nothing to do with the exchange part of the transaction, the American banking agent of the foreign lender turning over to the borrower not a sterling draft but the dollar proceeds of a sterling draft. How the exchange market fluctuates in the meantime--what rate may have to be paid at the end of ninety days for the necessary demand draft--concerns the borrower not at all. He received dollars in the first place, and when the loan comes due he pays back dollars, plus four, five or six per cent., as the case may be. What rate has to be paid for the demand exchange affects the banker only, not the borrower.

Loans made under the first conditions are known as sterling, mark, or franc loans; the other kind are usually called "currency loans." At the risk of repetition, it is to be said that in the case of sterling loans the borrower pays a flat commission and takes the risk of what rate he may have to pay for demand exchange when the loan comes due. In the case of a currency loan the borrower knows nothing about the foreign exchange transaction. He receives dollars, and pays them back with a fixed rate of interest, leaving the whole question and risk of exchange to the lending banker.

To illustrate the mechanism of one of these sterling loans. Suppose the London Bank, Ltd., to have arranged with the New York Bank to have the latter loan out ?00,000 in the New York market. The New York Bank draws ?00,000 of ninety days' sight bills, and, satisfactory collateral having been deposited, turns them over to the brokerage house of Smith & Jones. Smith & Jones at once sell the ?00,000, receiving therefor, say, $484,000.

The bills sold by Smith & Jones find their way to London by the first steamer, are accepted and discounted. Ninety days later they will come due and have to be paid, and ten days prior to their maturity the New York Bank will be expecting Smith & Jones to send in a demand draft for ?00,000, plus three-eighths per cent. commission, making ?75 additional. This ?00,375, less its commission for having handled the loan, the New York Bank will send to London, where it will arrive a couple of days before the ?00,000 of ninety days' sight bills originally drawn on the London Bank, Ltd., mature.

What each of the bankers concerned makes out of the transaction is plain enough. As to what Smith & Jones' ninety-day loan cost them, in addition to the flat three-eighths per cent. they had to pay, that depends upon what they realize from the sale of the ninety days' sight bills in the first place and secondly on what rate they had to pay for the demand bill for ?00,000. Exchange may have gone up during the life of the loan, making the loan expensive, or it may have gone down, making the cost very little. Plainly stated, unless they secured themselves by buying a "future" for the delivery of a ?00,000 demand bill in ninety days at a fixed rate, Messrs. Smith & Jones have been making a mild speculation in foreign exchange.

If the same loan had been made on the other basis, the New York Bank would have turned over to Smith & Jones not a sterling bill for ?00,000, but the dollar proceeds of such a bill, say a check for $484,000. At the end of ninety days Smith & Jones would have had to pay back $484,000, plus ninety days' interest at six per cent, $7,260, all of which cash, less commission, the New York Bank would have invested in a demand bill of exchange and sent over to the London Bank, Ltd. Whatever more than the ?00,000 needed to pay off the maturing nineties such a demand draft amounted to, would be the London Bank, Ltd.'s, profit.

From all of which it is plainly to be seen that when the London bankers are willing to lend money here and figure that the exchange market is on the down track, they will insist upon doing their lending on the "currency loan" basis--taking the risk of exchange themselves. Conversely, when loaning operations seem profitable but rates seem to be on the upturn, lenders will do their best to put their money out in the form of "sterling loans." Bankers are not always right in their views, by any means, but as a general principle it can be said that when big amounts of foreign money offered in this market are all offered on the "sterling loan" basis, a rising exchange market is to be expected.

As to the collateral on these foreign loans, it is evident that there is as much chance for different ways of looking at different stocks as there is in regular domestic loaning operations. Not only does the standing of the borrower here make a difference, but there are certain securities which certain banks abroad favor, and others, perhaps just as good, with which they will have nothing to do.

Excepting the case of special negotiation, however, it may be said that the collateral put up the case of foreign loans in this market is of a very high order. Three years ago this could hardly have been said, but one of the many beneficial effects of the panic was to greatly raise the standard of the collateral required by foreign lenders in this market. It used formerly to be more a case of the standing of the borrower. Nowadays the collateral is usually deposited here in care of a banker or trust company.

From what has been said about the mechanism of making these foreign loans, it is evident that no transfer of cash actually takes place, and that what really happens is that the foreign banking institution lends out its credit instead of its cash. For in no case is the lender required to put up any money. The drafts drawn upon him are at ninety days' sight, and all he has to do is to write the word "accepted," with his signature, across their face. Later they will be presented for actual payment, but by that time the "cover" will have reached London from the banker in America who drew the "nineties," and the maturing bills will be paid out of that. The foreign lender, in other words, is at no stage out of any actual capital, although it is true, of course, that he has obligated himself to pay the drafts on maturity, by "accepting" them.

Where, then, is the limit of what the foreign bankers can lend in the New York market? On one consideration only does that depend--the amount of accepted long bills which the London discount market will stand. For all the ninety days' sight bills drawn in the course of these transfers of credit must eventually be discounted in the London discount market, and when the London discount market refuses to absorb bills of this kind a material check is naturally administered to their creation.

Too great drawings of loan-bills, as the long bills drawn to make foreign loans are called, are quickly reflected in a squeamish London discount market. It needs only the refusal of the Bank of England to re-discount the paper of a few London banks suspected of having "accepted" too great a quantity of American loan-bills, to make it impossible to go on loaning profitably in the New York market. In order to make loans, long bills have to be drawn and sold to somebody, and if the discount market in London will take no more American paper, buyers for freshly-created American paper will be hard to find.

To get back to the part foreign loaning operations play in the foreign exchange market here, it is plain that as no actual money is put up, the business is attractive and profitable to the bank having the requisite facilities and the right foreign connection. It means the putting of the bank's name on a good deal of paper, it is true, but only on the deposit of entirely satisfactory collateral and only in connection with the assuming of the same obligation by a foreign institution of high standing. There are few instances where loss in transacting this form of business has been sustained, while the profits derived from it are very large.

As to what the foreign department of an American bank makes out of the business, it may be said that that depends very largely upon whether the bank here acts merely as a lending agent or whether the operation is for "joint account," both as to risk and commission. In the former case (and more and more this seems to be becoming the basis on which the business is done) both the American and the European bank stands to make a very fair return-- always considering that neither is called upon to put up one real dollar or pound sterling. Take, for instance, the average sterling loan made on the basis of the borrower taking all the risk of exchange and paying a flat commission of three-eighths of one per cent. for each ninety days. That means that each bank makes three-sixteenths of one per cent. for every ninety days the loan runs--the American bank for simply drawing its ninety-day bills of exchange and the English bank for merely accepting them. Naturally, competition is keen, American banking houses vying with each other both for the privilege of acting as agents of the foreign banks having money to lend, and of going into joint-account loaning operations with them. Three-sixteenths or perhaps one-quarter of one per cent. for ninety days (three-quarters of one per cent. and one per cent. annually) may not seem much of an inducement, but considering the fact that no real cash is involved, this percentage is enough to make the biggest and best banking houses in the country go eagerly after the business.

5. The Drawing of Finance-Bills

Approaching the subject of finance-bills, the author is well aware that concerning this phase of the foreign exchange business there is wide difference of opinion. Finance bills make money, but they make trouble, too. Their existence is one of the chief points of contact between the foreign exchange and the other markets, and one of the principal reasons why a knowledge of foreign exchange is necessary to any well-rounded understanding of banking conditions.

Strictly speaking, a finance-bill is a long draft drawn by a banker of one country on a banker in another, sometimes secured by collateral, but more often not, and issued by the drawing banker for the purpose of raising money. Such bills are not always distinguishable from the bills a banker in New York may draw on a banker in London in the operation of lending money for him, but in nature they are essentially different. The drawing of finance-bills was recently described by the foreign exchange manager of one of the biggest houses in New York, during the course of a public address, as a "scheme to raise the wind." Whether or not any collateral is put up, the whole purpose of the drawing of finance-bills is to provide an easy way of raising money without the banker here having to go to some other bank to do it.

The origin of the ordinary finance-bill is about as follows: A bank here in New York carries a good balance in London and works a substantial foreign exchange business in connection with the London bank where this balance is carried. A time comes when the New York banking house could advantageously use more money. Arrangements are therefore made with the London bank whereby the London bank agrees to "accept" a certain amount of the American banker's long bills, for a commission. In the course of his regular business, then, the American banker simply draws that many more pounds sterling in long bills, sells them, and for the time being has the use of the money. In the great majority of cases no extra collateral is put up, nor is the London bank especially secured in any way. The American banker's credit is good enough to make the English banker willing, for a commission, to "accept" his drafts and obligate himself that the drafts will be paid at maturity. Naturally, a house has to be in good standing and enjoy high credit not only here but on the other side before any reputable London bank can be induced to "accept" its finance paper.

The ability to draw finance-bills of this kind often puts a house disposed to take chances with the movement of the exchange market into line for very considerable profit possibilities. Suppose, for instance, that the manager of a house here figures that there is going to be a sharp break in foreign exchange. He, therefore, sells a line of ninety-day bills, putting himself technically short of the exchange market and banking on the chance of being able to buy in his "cover" cheaply when it comes time for him to cover. In the meantime he has the use of the money he derived from the sale of the "nineties" to do with as he pleases, and if he has figured the market aright, it may not cost him any more per pound to buy his "cover" than he realized from the sale of the long bills. In which case he would have had the use of the money for the whole three months practically free of interest.

It is plain speculating in exchange--there is no getting away from it, and yet this practice of selling finance-bills gives such an opportunity to the exchange manager shrewd enough to read the situation aright to make money, that many of the big houses go in for it to a large extent. During the summer, for instance, if the outlook is for big crops, the situation is apt to commend itself to this kind of operation. Money in the summer months is apt to be low and exchange high, affording a good basis on which to sell exchange. Then, if the expected crops materialize, large amounts of exchange drawn against exports will come into the market, forcing down rates and giving the operator who has previously sold his long bills an excellent chance to cover them profitably as they come due.

About the best example of how exchange managers can be deceived in their forecasts is afforded by the movement of exchange during the summer and fall of 1909. Impelled thereto by the brilliant crop prospects of early summer, foreign exchange houses in New York drew and sold finance-bills in enormous volume. The corn crop was to run over three billion bushels, affording an unprecedented exportable surplus--wheat and cotton were both to show record-breaking yields. But instead of these promises being fulfilled, wheat and corn showed only average yields, while the cotton crop turned out decidedly short. The expected flood of exchange never materialized. On the contrary, rise in money rates abroad caused such a paying off of foreign loans and maturing finance bills that foreign exchange rose to the gold export point and "covering" operations were conducted with extreme difficulty. In the foreign exchange market the autumn of 1909 will long be remembered as a time when the finance-bill sellers had administered to them a lesson which they will be a good while in forgetting.

6. Arbitraging in Exchange

Arbitraging in exchange--the buying by a New York banker, for instance, through the medium of the London market, of exchange drawn on Paris, is another broad and profitable field for the operations of the expert foreign exchange manager. Take, for example, a time when exchange on Paris is more plentiful in London than in New York--a shrewd New York exchange manager needing a draft on Paris might well secure it in London rather than in his home city. The following operation is only one of ten thousand in which exchange men are continually engaged, but is a representative transaction and one on which a good deal of the business in the arbitration of exchange is based.

Suppose, for instance, that in New York, demand exchange on Paris is quoted at five francs seventeen and one-half centimes per dollar, demand exchange on London at $4.84 per pound, and that, in London, exchange on Paris is obtainable at twenty-five francs twenty-five centimes per pound. The following operation would be possible:

Sale by a New York banker of a draft on Paris, say, for francs 25,250, at 5.17-1/2, bringing him in $4,879.23. Purchase by same banker of a draft on London for ?,000, at 4.84, costing him $4,840. Instructions by the American banker to his London correspondent to buy a check on Paris for francs 25,250 in London, and to send it over to Paris for the credit of his (the American banker's account). Such a draft, at 25.25 would cost just ?,000.

The circle would then be complete. The American banker who originally drew the francs 25,250 on his Paris balance would have replaced that amount in his Paris balance through the aid of his London correspondent. The London correspondent would have paid out ?,000 from the American banker's balance with him, a draft for which amount would come in the next mail. All parties to the transaction would be satisfied--especially the banker who started it, for whereas he paid out $4,840 for the ?,000 draft on London, he originally took in $4,879.23 for the draft he sold on Paris.

Between such cities as have been used in the foregoing illustrations rates are not apt to be wide enough apart to afford any such actual profit, but the chance for arbitraging does exist and is being continuously taken advantage of. So keenly, indeed, are the various rates in their possible relation to one another watched by the exchange men that it is next to impossible for them to "open up" to any appreciable extent. The chance to make even a slight profit by shifting balances is so quickly availed of that in the constant demand for exchange wherever any relative weakness is shown, there exists a force which keeps the whole structure at parity. The ability to buy drafts on Paris relatively much cheaper at London than at New York, for instance, would be so quickly taken advantage of by half a dozen watchful exchange men that the London rate on Paris would quickly enough be driven up to its right relative position.

It is impossible in this brief treatise to give more than a suggestion of the various kinds of exchange arbitration being carried on all the time. Experts do not confine their operations to the main centers, nor is three necessarily the largest number of points which figure in transactions of this sort. Elaborate cable codes and a constant use of the wires keep the up-to-date exchange manager in touch with the movement of rates in every part of Europe. If a chance exists to sell a draft on London and then to put the requisite balance there through an arbitration involving Paris, Brussels, and Amsterdam, the chances are that there will be some shrewd manager who will find it out and put through the transaction. Some of the larger banking houses employ men who do little but look for just such opportunities. When times are normal, the margin of profit is small, but in disturbed markets the parities are not nearly so closely maintained and substantial profits are occasionally made. The business, however, is of the most difficult character, requiring not only great shrewdness and judgment but exceptional mechanical facilities.

7. Dealing in "Futures"

As a means of making--or of losing--money, in the foreign exchange business, the dealing in contracts for the future delivery of exchange has, perhaps, no equal. And yet trading in futures is by no means necessarily speculation. There are at least two broad classes of legitimate operation in which the buying and selling of contracts of exchange for future delivery plays a vital part.

Take the case of a banker who has bought and remitted to his foreign correspondent a miscellaneous lot of foreign exchange made up to the extent of one-half, perhaps, of commercial long bills with documents deliverable only on "payment" of the draft. That means that if the whole batch of exchange amounted to ?0,000, ?5,000 of it might not become an available balance on the other side for a good while after it had arrived there--not until the parties on whom the "payment" bills were drawn chose to pay them off under rebate. The exchange rate, in the meantime, might do almost anything, and the remitting banker might at the end of thirty or forty-five days find himself with a balance abroad on which he could sell his checks only at very low rates.

To protect himself in such case the banker would, at the time he sent over the commercial exchange, sell his own demand drafts for future delivery. Suppose that he had sent over ?5,000 of commercial "payment" bills. Unable to tell exactly when the proceeds would become available, the banker buying the bills would nevertheless presumably have had experience with bills of the same name before and would be able to form a pretty accurate estimate as to when the drawees would be likely to "take them up" under rebate. It would be reasonably safe, for instance, for the banker to sell futures as follows: ?,000 deliverable in fifteen days; ?0,000 deliverable in thirty days, ?0,000 deliverable in from forty-five to sixty days. Such drafts on being presented could in all probability be taken care of out of the prepayments on the commercial bills.

By figuring with judgment, foreign exchange bankers are often able to make substantial profits on operations of this kind. An exchange broker comes in and offers a banker here a lot of good "payment" commercial bills. The banker finds that he can sell his own draft for delivery at about the time the commercial drafts are apt to be paid under rebate, at a price which means a good net profit. The operation ties up capital, it is true, but is without risk. Not infrequently good commercial "payment" bills can be bought at such a price and bankers' futures sold against them at such a price that there is a substantial profit to be made.

The other operation is the sale of bankers' futures, not against remittances of actual commercial exchange but against exporters' futures. Exporters of merchandise frequently quote prices to customers abroad for shipment to be made in some following month, to establish which fixed price the exporter has to fix a rate of exchange definitely with some banker. "I am going to ship so-and-so so many tubs of lard next May," says the exporter to the banker, "the drafts against them will amount to so-and-so-much. What rate will you pay me for them--delivery next May?" The banker knows he can sell his own draft for May delivery for, say, 4.87. He bids the exporter 4.86-1/2 for his lard bills, and gets the contract. Without any risk and without tying up a dollar of capital the banker has made one-half cent per pound sterling on the whole amount of the shipment. In May, the lard bills will come in to him, and he will pay for them at a rate of 4.86-1/2, turning around and delivering his own draft against them at 4.87.

Selling futures against futures is not the easiest form of foreign exchange business to put through, but when a house has a large number of commercial exporters among its clients there are generally to be found among them some who want to sell their exchange for future delivery. As to the buyer of the banker's "future," such a buyer might be, for instance, another banker who had sold finance-bills and wants to limit the cost of "covering" them.

The foregoing examples of dealing in futures are merely examples of how futures may figure in every-day exchange transactions. Like operations in exchange arbitrage, there is no limit to the number of kinds of business in which "futures" may figure. They are a much abused institution, but are a vital factor in modern methods of transacting foreign exchange business.

The foregoing are the main forms of activity of the average foreign department, though there are, of course, many other ways of making money out of foreign exchange. The business of granting commercial credits, the exporting and importing of gold and the business of international trading in securities will be taken up separately in following chapters.

CHAPTER VII

GOLD EXPORTS AND IMPORTS

Gold exports and imports, while not constituting any great part of the activity of the average foreign department, are nevertheless a factor of vital importance in determining the movement of exchange. The loss of gold, in quantity, by some market may bring about money conditions resulting in very violent movements of exchange; or, on the other hand, such movements may be caused by the efforts of the controlling financial interests in some market to attract gold. The movement of exchange and the movement of gold are absolutely dependent one on the other.

Considering broadly this question of the movement of gold, it is to be borne in mind that by far the greater part of the world's production of the precious metal takes place in countries ranking very low as to banking importance. The United States, is indeed, the only first-class financial power in which any very considerable proportion of the world's gold is produced. Excepting the ninety million dollars of gold produced in the United States in 1908, nearly all of the total production of 430 million dollars for that year was taken out of the ground in places where there exists but the slightest demand for it for use in banking or the arts.

That being the case, it follows that there is to be considered, first, the primary movement of nearly all the gold produced--the movement from the mines to the great financial centers.

Considering that over half the gold taken out of the ground each year is mined in British possessions, it is only natural that London should be the greatest distributive point. Such is the case. Ownership of the mines which produce most of the world's gold is held in London, and so it is to the British capital that most of the world's gold comes after it has been taken out of the ground. By every steamer arriving from Australia and South Africa great quantities of the metal are carried to London, there to be disposed of at the best price available.

For raw gold, like raw copper or raw iron, has a price. Under the English banking law, it is true, the Bank of England must buy at the rate of seventy-seven shillings nine pence per ounce all the gold of standard (.916-2/3) fineness which may be offered it, but that establishes merely a minimum--there is no limit the other way to which the price of the metal may not be driven under sufficiently urgent bidding.

The distribution of the raw gold is effected as follows: Each Monday morning there is held an auction at which are present all the representatives of home or foreign banks who may be in the market for gold. These representatives, fully apprised of the amount of the metal which has arrived during the preceding week and which is to be sold, know exactly how much they can bid. The gold, therefore, is sold at the best possible price, and finds its way to that point where the greatest urgency of demand exists. It may be Paris or Berlin, or it may be the Bank of England. According as the representatives present at the auction may bid, the disposition of the gold is determined.

The primary disposition. For the fact that Berlin, for instance, obtains the bulk of the gold auctioned off on any given Monday by no means proves that the gold is going to remain for any length of time in Berlin. For some reason, in that particular case, the representatives of the German banks had been instructed to bid a price for the gold which would bring it to Berlin, but the conditions furnishing the motive for such a move may remain operative only a short time and the need for the metal pass away with them. Quarterly settlements in Berlin or the flotation of a Russian loan in Paris, for instance, might be enough to make the German and French banks' representatives go in and bid high enough to get the new gold, but with the passing of the quarter's end or the successful launching of the loan would pass the necessity for the gold, and its re-distribution would begin.

In other words, both the primary movement of gold from the mines and the secondary movement from the distributive centers are merely temporary and show little as to the final lodgment of the precious metal. What really counts is exchange conditions; it is along the lines of the favorable exchange that the great currents of gold will inevitably flow.

For example, if a draft for pounds sterling drawn on London can be bought here at a low rate of exchange, anything in London that the American consumer may want to possess himself of can be bought cheaper than when exchange on London is high. The price of a hat in London is, say, ?. With exchange at 4.83 it will cost a buyer in New York only $4.83 to buy that hat; if exchange were at 4.88, it would cost him $4.88. Similarly with raw copper or raw gold or any other commodity. Given a low rate of exchange on any point and it is possible for the outside markets to buy cheaply at that point.

And a very little difference in the price of exchange makes a very great difference so far as the price of gold is concerned. As stated in a previous chapter, a new gold sovereign at any United States assay office can be converted into $4.8665, so that if it cost nothing to bring a new sovereign over here, no one holding a draft for a pound (a sovereign is a gold pound) would sell it for less than $4.8665, but would simply order the sovereign sent over here and cash it in for $4.8665 himself. Always assuming that it cost nothing to bring over the actual gold, every time it became possible to buy a draft for less than $4.8665, some buyer would snatch at the chance.

Such a case, with ? as the amount of the draft and the assumption of no charge for importing the gold, is, of course, mentioned merely for purposes of illustration. From it should, however, become clear the whole idea underlying gold imports. A new sovereign laid down in New York is worth, at any time, $4.8665. If it is possible to get the sovereign over here for less than that--by paying $4.83 for a ? draft on London, for instance, and three cents for charges, $4.86 in all--it is possible to bring the sovereign in and make money doing it.

Whether the gold imported is in the form of sovereigns or whether it consists of bars makes not the slightest difference so far as the principle of the thing is concerned. A sovereign is at all times worth just so and so much at any United States assay office, and an ounce of gold of any given fineness is worth just so and so much, too, regardless of where it comes from. So that in importing gold, whether the metal be in the form of coin or bars, the great thing is the cheapness with which it can be secured in some foreign market. If it can be secured so cheaply in London, for example, that the price paid for each pound (sovereign) of the draft, plus the charge of bringing in each sovereign, is less than what the sovereign can be sold for when it gets here, it will pay to buy English gold and bring it in.

Exactly the same principle applies where the question is of importing gold bars instead of sovereigns, except that bars cannot be bought in London at a fixed rate. That, however, in no way affects the underlying principle that in importing gold the profit is made by selling the gold here for more dollars than the combined dollar-cost of the draft on London with which the gold is bought and the charges incurred in importing the metal. To illustrate, if the draft cost $997,000 and the charges amounted to $3,000, the gold (whether in the form of sovereigns, eagles or bars) would have to be sold here for at least $1,000,000, to have the importer come out even.

With exports, the theory of the thing is to sell a draft on, say, London, for more dollars than the dollar-cost of enough gold, plus charges, to meet the draft. As will be seen from the figures of an actual shipment, given further on, the banker who ships gold gets the money to buy the gold from the Treasury here, by selling a sterling draft on London. Suppose, for example, a New York banker wants to create a ?00,000 balance in London. Figuring how many ounces of gold (at the buying price in London) will give him the ?00,000 credit, he buys that much gold and sends it over. Suppose the combined cost of the gold and the charge for shipping it amounts to $976,000. If the banker here can sell a ?00,000 draft against it at 4.88, he will just get back the $976,000 he laid out originally and be even on the transaction.

Before passing from the theory to the practice of gold exports and imports, there is to be considered the fact that bar gold sells in London at a constantly varying price, while in New York it sells at a definitely fixed price. In New York an ounce of gold of any given fineness can always be sold for the same amount of dollars and cents, but in London the amount of shillings and pence into which it is convertible varies constantly. So that a New York banker figuring on bringing in bar gold from London has to take carefully into account what the price per ounce of bar gold over there is. Sovereigns are seldom imported because they are secured in London not by weight but by face value,--even if the sovereigns have lost weight they cost just as many pounds sterling to secure. Where the New York banker is exporting gold, on the other hand, the price at which bar gold is selling in London is just as important as where he is importing. For the price at which the gold can be disposed of when it gets to London determines into how many pounds sterling it can be converted.

These matters of the cost of gold in one market and the crediting of the gold in some other market are not the easiest thing to grasp at first thought, but will perhaps become quite clear by reference to the accompanying calculation of actual gold export and gold import transactions. All the way through it must be remembered that the figures of such calculations can never be absolute--that insurance and freight charges vary and that different operations are conducted along different lines. The two operations described embody, however, the principle of both the outward and inward movement of bar gold at New York.

Export of Bars to London

In the transaction described below about a quarter of a million dollars' worth of bar gold is shipped to London, the money to pay for the gold being raised by the drawing and selling of a demand draft on London. Assuming that the draft is drawn and the gold shipped at the same time, the draft will be presented fully three days before the gold is credited, that being the time necessary for assaying, weighing, etc. In other words, there will be an "overdraft" for at least three days, interest on which will have to be figured as a part of the cost of the operation.

Following is the detailed statement:

13,195-1/2 ounces bar gold (.9166 fine) purchased from U.S. Treasury or Sub-Treasury at $18.9459 per ounce $250,000

Assay office charge (4 cents per $100) 100

Cartage and packing 20

Freight (5/32 per cent.) 390

Insurance (1/20 per cent.) 125

Interest on overdraft in London (from time draft has to be paid until the gold is credited) 3 days at 4 per cent. 83 --------- Total expense of buying and shipping the gold $250,718

13,195-1/2 ounces of gold credited in London at 77 shillings 10-1/2 pence ?1,380

Draft on London for ?1,380, sold by shipper of the gold, at 487.96 $250,718

In the transaction described above, the "overdraft" caused by the inevitable delay in assaying and weighing the gold on its arrival in London lasted for three days, the American banker being charged interest at the rate of four per cent. 487.96 being the rate at which the banker exporting the gold was able to sell his demand draft at the time, was, under those conditions, the "gold export point."

In this particular operation, which was undertaken purely for advertising purposes, the shipper of the gold came out exactly even. Suppose, however, that he had been able to sell his draft, against the gold shipped, at 4.88 instead of 4.87-3/4. That would have meant twenty-five points (one-quarter cent per pound) more, which, on ?1,380, would have amounted to $128.25.

This question of the profit on gold exports is both interesting and, because it has a strong bearing at times on the question of whether or not to ship gold, important. No rule can be laid down as to what profit bankers expect to make on shipments. If, for instance, a banker owes ?00,000 abroad himself and finds it cheaper to send gold than to buy a bill, the question of profit does not enter at all. Then, again, many and many an export transaction is induced by ulterior motives--it may be for the sake of advertising, or for stock market purposes, or because some correspondent abroad needs the gold and is willing to pay for it. Any one of these or many like reasons may explain the phenomenon, occasionally seen, of gold exports at a time when conditions plainly indicate that the exporter is shipping at a loss.

As a rule, however, when exchange is scarce and the demand so great that bankers who do not themselves owe money abroad see a chance to supply the demand for exchange by shipping gold and drawing drafts against it, the profit amounts to anywhere from $400 to $1,000 on each million dollars shipped--for less than the first amount named it is hardly worth while to go into the transaction at all; on the other hand, conditions have to be pretty much disordered to force exchange to a point where the larger amount named can be earned.

Import of Bars from London

Turning now to the discussion of the conditions under which gold is imported, it will appear from the following calculation that interest plays a much more important part in the case of gold imports than in the case of exports. With exports, as has been shown, the interest charge is merely on a three days' overdraft, but in the case of imports the banker who brings in the gold loses interest on it for the whole time it is in transit and for a day or two on each end, besides. A New York banker, carrying a large balance in London, for instance, orders his London correspondent to buy and ship him a certain amount of bar gold. This the London banker does, charging the cost of the metal, and all shipping charges, to the account of the New York banker. On the whole amount thus charged, therefore, the New York banker loses interest while the gold is afloat. Even after the gold arrives in New York, of course, the depleted balance abroad continues to draw less interest than formerly, but to make up for that the gold begins to earn interest as soon as it gets here.

The transaction given below is one which was made under the above conditions--the importer in New York had a good balance in London and ordered his London correspondent to buy and ship about $1,000,000 of gold, charging the cost and all expenses to his (the New York banker's) account. In this particular case the interest lost in London was at six per cent. and lasted for ten days.

Cost in the London market of 52,782 ounces of gold (.9166 fine) at 77 shillings, 11-3/4 pence per ounce ?05,795

Freight (5/32 per cent.) 320

Insurance 102

Boxing and carting 9

Commission for buying the gold 26

Interest on cost of gold and on charges, while gold is in transit, 10 days at 6 per cent. 343 ---------- ?06,595

Proceeds, at U.S. Sub-Treasury in New York, of the 52,782 ounces of gold at $18.9459 per ounce $1,000,000

$1,000,000 invested in a cable on London at $484.04 ?06,595

In the above calculation it will be seen that the proceeds of the gold imported were exactly enough to buy a cable on London sufficiently large to cancel the original outlay for the gold and the expenses incurred in shipping it over here. On the whole transaction the banker importing the gold came out exactly even; a trifle over 4.84 was the "gold import point" at the time.

In a general way it can be said that the profit made on gold import operations is less than where gold is exported. Banking houses big enough and strong enough to engage in business of this character are more apt to be on the constructive side of the market than on the other, and will frequently bring in gold at no profit to themselves, or even at a loss, in order to further their plans. It does happen, of course, that gold is sometimes shipped out for stock market effect, but the effect of gold exports is growing less and less. Gold imports, on the other hand, are always a stimulating factor and are good live stock market ammunition as well as a constructive argument regarding the price of investments in general.

Exports of Gold Bars to Paris--the "Triangular Operation"

Calculations have been given regarding the movement of bar gold between London and New York--what is ordinarily known as the "direct" movement.

"Indirect" movements, however, have figured so prominently of recent years in the exchange market that at least one example ought perhaps to be given. Far and away the most important of such "indirect movements" are those in which gold is shipped from New York to Paris for the sake of creating a credit balance in London.

Before examining the actual figures of such an operation it may be well to glance at the theory of the thing. A New York banker, say, for any one of many different reasons, wants to create a credit balance in London. Examining exchange conditions, he finds that sterling drafts drawn on London are to be had relatively cheaper in Paris than in New York. In the natural course of exchange arbitrage the New York banker would therefore buy a draft on Paris and send it to his French correspondent with instruction to use it to buy a draft on London and to remit such draft to London for credit of his (the American banker's) account.

But exchange on Paris is not always plentiful in the New York market, and very likely the New York banker will find that if he wants to send anything to Paris he will have to send gold. Assume, then, that he finds conditions favorable and decides to thus transfer a couple of hundred thousand pounds to London by sending gold to Paris. The operation might work out as follows:

Cost of 48,500 ounces of bar gold (.995 fine) at U.S. Sub-Treasury, New York, at $20.5684 per ounce $997,567

Insurance (4-1/2 cents per $100) 450

Freight (5/32 per cent.) 1,555

Assay office charges (4 cents per $100) 400

Cartage and packing 60

Commission in Paris 250

Interest from time gold is shipped from New York until draft on new credit in London can be safely drawn and sold, 6 daysat 2 per cent. 333 ----------- $1,000,615

The gold arrives in Paris and is bought by the Bank of France--

48,500 ounces at fcs. 106.3705 per ounce, equals fcs. 5,158,969

That amount of francs then invested in a check on London, and the check sent to London for credit of the American banker, fcs. 5,158,969 at 25 francs 10 centimes per ??05,536

New York banker sells his draft on London for ?05,536 at 4.86832 $1,000,615

Conditions principally affecting the shipment of gold by the triangular operation, it will be seen from the above calculation, are the rate of exchange on London at New York, and the rate of exchange on London at Paris. The higher the rate at which the New York banker can sell his bills on London after the gold has been shipped, the more money he will make. The lower the rate at which his Paris agent can secure the drafts drawn on London, the greater the amount of pounds sterling which the gold will buy. High sterling exchange in New York and low sterling exchange in Paris are therefore the main features of the combination of circumstances which result in these "triangular operations."

Gold Shipments to Argentina

Of the many other ways in which gold moves, one way seems to be becoming so increasingly important that it is well worthy of attention. Reference is made to the shipment of gold from New York to the Argentine for account of English bankers who have debts to discharge there.

Owing to Argentine loans placed in the English market and to heavy exports of wheat, hides, and meat from Buenos Aires to London, there exists almost a chronic condition of indebtedness on the part of the London bankers to the bankers in the Argentine. Not offset by any corresponding imports, these conditions are putting Buenos Aires each year in a better and better condition to make heavy demands upon London for gold, demands which have recently grown to such an extent as to make serious inroads on the British banks' reserves. Unwilling to comply with this demand for gold, the powers in charge of the London market have on several occasions deliberately produced money conditions in London resulting in a shifting of the Argentine demand for gold upon New York. The means by which this has been accomplished has been the raising of the Bank of England rate to a point sufficiently high to make the dollar-exchange on New York fall. Able, then, to buy dollar-drafts on New York very cheaply, the London bankers send to New York large amounts of such drafts, with instructions that they be used to buy gold for shipment to the Argentine.

The very general confusion of mind regarding these operations in gold comes perhaps from the fact that they are constantly referred to as being a result of high exchange on London, at New York. Which is true, but a most misleading way of expressing the fact that low exchange on New York, at London, is the reason of the shipments. High sterling exchange at New York and low dollar-exchange at London are, of course, one and the same thing. But in this case, what counts is that dollar-exchange can be cheaply bought in London.

No attempt is made in this little work to cover the whole field of operations in gold, infinite in scope as they are and of every conceivable variety. But from the examples given above it ought to be possible to work out a fairly clear idea as to why gold exports and imports take place and as to what the conditions are which bring them about.

While not failing to realize the importance to the markets of the movement back and forth of great amounts of gold, it may nevertheless be said that from the standpoint of the foreign exchange business the importance of transactions in gold is very generally overestimated. Most dealers in foreign exchange steer clear of exporting or importing gold whenever they can, the business being practically all done by half-a-dozen firms and banks. As has been seen, the profit to be made is miserably small as a rule, while the trouble and risk are very considerable. Import operations, especially, tie up large amounts of ready capital and often throw the regular working of a foreign department out of gear for days and even weeks. There is considerable newspaper advertising to be had by being always among the first to ship or bring in gold, but there are a good many houses who do not want or need that kind of advertising. Some of the best and strongest banking houses in New York, indeed, make it a rule to have nothing to do with operations in gold one way or the other. Should they need drafts on the other side at a time when there are no drafts to be had, such houses prefer to let some one else do the gold-shipping and are willing to let the shipping house make its one-sixteenth of one per cent. or one-thirty-second of one per cent. in the rate of exchange it charges for the bills drawn against the gold.

Particular attention has been paid all through the foregoing chapter to the gold movement in its relation to the New York markets, the movement between foreign points being too big a subject to describe in a work of this kind. In general, however, it can be said that of the three great gold markets abroad, London is the only one which can in any sense be called "free." In Paris, the ability of the Bank of France to pay its notes in silver instead of gold makes it possible for the Bank of France to control the gold movement absolutely, while in Germany the paternalistic attitude of the government is so insistent that gold exports are rarely undertaken by bankers except with the full sanction of the governors of the Reichsbank.

It is a question, even, whether London makes good its boast of maintaining Europe's only "free" gold market. The new gold coming from the mines does, it is true, find its way to London, for the purpose of being auctioned off to the highest bidder, but as the kind of bids which can be made are governed so largely by arbitrary action on the part of the Bank of England, it is a question whether the gold auction can be said to be "free." Suppose, for instance, that the "Old Lady of Threadneedle Street" decides that enough gold has been taken by foreign bidders and that exports had better be checked. Instantly the bank rate goes up, making it harder for the representatives of the foreign banks to bid. Should the rise in the rate not be sufficient to affect the outside exchange on London, the Bank will probably resort to the further expedient of entering the auction for its own account and outbidding all others. Not having any shipping charges to pay on this gold it buys, the Bank is usually able to secure all the gold it wants--or, rather, to keep anybody else from securing it. The auction is open to all, it is true, but being at times conducted under such circumstances, is hardly a market which can be called "free."

If there is any "free" gold market in the world, indeed, it is to be found in the United States. All anybody who wants gold, in this country, has to do, is to go around to the nearest sub-treasury and get it. If the supply of bars is exhausted, the buyer may be disappointed, but that has nothing to do with any restriction on the market. The market for gold bars in the United States is at the Treasury and the various sub-treasuries, and as long as the prospective buyer has the legal tender to offer, he can buy the gold bars which may be on hand. And at a fixed price, regardless of how urgent the demand may be, who he is, or who else may be bidding. First come first served is the rule, and a rule which is observed as long as the bars hold out. After that, whoever still wants gold can take it in the form of coin.

How such conditions have worked out, so far as our gaining or losing gold is concerned, can be seen from the following table, introduced here for the purpose of giving a clear idea as to just where the United States has stood in the international movement of gold during the five-year period given below:

Exports of Excess of Gold from U.S. Imports Imports

	Exports	Imports	Excess of Gold from U.S.
1913	$77,762,622	$69,194,025	[1]$8,568,597
1912	57,328,348	48,936,500	[1]8,391,848
1911	22,509,653	73,607,013	51,097,360
1910	118,563,215	43,339,905	[1]75,223,310
1909	91,531,818	44,003,989	[1]47,527,829

[1] Excess of exports

In conclusion, it may be said that the prediction that as international financial relationships between banks are drawn closer, gold movements will tend to decrease, seem hardly to be borne out by the figures of the table given above. Banks here and banks abroad are working together in a way unknown ten or even five years ago, but as yet there are no signs of any lessening in the inward or outward movement of specie. More liberal granting of international credits, increased international loaning operations, far from putting an end to the physical movement of gold in large quantities,--these are influences tending to make gold move more freely than ever. The day of the treasure galleons is over, but in their place we have swift-moving steamers by which gold can be shifted from one point to another with safety and ease. Gold movements seem as though they were to play an important part in the markets for a good many years to come.

CHAPTER VIII

FOREIGN EXCHANGE IN ITS RELATION TO INTERNATIONAL SECURITY TRADING

On account of the huge fixed investment of foreign money in the United States, on account of Europe's continuous speculative interest in our markets, and the activity of the "arbitrageurs" in both bonds and shares, dealings in securities between ourselves and the Old World are always on a very great scale. Not infrequently, indeed, Europe's position on American securities is an influence of dominating importance.

From the maturities, refunding operations, and interest remittances alone, growing out of the permanent investment of foreign money in our securities, there results a very great amount of international security and exchange business. Whether Europe's investment here amounts to three billions or four billions or five billions, it is impossible to say; the fact remains that it is so large that every year a very great amount of foreign-held bonds come due and have to be paid off or refunded, and, further, that the remitting abroad of coupon and dividend money each year calls for upward of $150,000,000.

This matter of maturing investments, alone, calls for continuous international security trading and on a large scale. Each year there comes due in this country an amount of railroad and other bonds running well up into the hundreds of millions, of which a large proportion are held on the other side. Some of these maturities are paid off in cash--more often, refunding bonds are offered in exchange; seldom, indeed, are the maturing investments allowed to remain unreplaced. European investors, especially, have consistently done well with money placed in this country, and the running off to maturity of a foreign-held American bond is nearly sure to be followed up by replacement with some other American security.

Bond houses doing an international business are therefore keenly watchful of the maturity of issues largely held abroad, and are ever ready with offers of new and attractive investments. Knowledge of the location of American investments in Europe is thus a business asset of the greatest importance, and records are carefully kept. The fact that a dealer here knows that some bank in London has a wealthy client who holds a big block of certain bonds about to mature, may very possibly mean that the house here may be able to make a very profitable trade. Information of this character is carefully gathered wherever possible and as carefully guarded. The longer a house has been in business, naturally, and the closer its financial relationship with investment interests abroad, the more of this sort of information it is bound to possess.

Foreign exchange growing out of these renewals and refundings is on a very large scale. Sometimes the placing of a new issue abroad means such immediate drawing of drafts on foreign buyers of the securities as to depress the exchange market sharply. Sometimes, as in the case of new issues of railroad stock, where payments are usually made in instalments covering a year or more, the drawing of exchange is distributed in such a way that its influence, if felt at all, is felt merely as an underlying element of weakness.

Of a somewhat different character are the foreign exchange transactions originating from what might be called Europe's "floating" investment in American securities and from the out-and-out speculations carried on in this market by the foreigners.

There is never a time, probably, when the floating foreign investment in American stocks and bonds does not run up with the hundreds of millions of dollars. "Speculation," such operations would probably be called by many people, but whether speculation or not, a form of activity which is continually giving rise to big dealings in foreign exchange. For this "floating" investment is very largely for account of bankers whose international connections and credit make it possible for them to carry stocks and bonds through the agency of the exchange market, and without having to put up any actual money. The ingenious method by which this is accomplished is about as follows:

A banker here, for instance, decides that a certain low-priced bond is cheap and that if purchased it will show a substantial profit within six months or a year. Not wanting to buy the bonds and borrow on them here, he invites his foreign correspondent into the deal on joint account, arranging to raise the money with which to buy the bonds by drawing a ninety-day sight draft on the foreign correspondent. This he does, drawing, say, a ?0,000 draft at ninety days' sight, and selling it in the exchange market at, let us say, $4.83.

The $241,500 received from the sale of the draft, the American banker uses to buy the bonds. Ninety days later the draft will come due in London, and have to be covered (or renewed) from this side, but in the meantime, a profitable chance to sell the bonds may present itself. If not, the draft can be "renewed" at the end of the ninety days, and again and again if necessary, until the bankers are willing to close out the bonds.

This operation of "renewing" long drafts drawn for the purpose of carrying securities is one of the most interesting phases of foreign exchange business in connection with international security dealings. The draft has been drawn, say, for ?0,000. The end of the ninety-day period comes, the draft is due, is presented, and has to be paid. But the bankers do not choose to sell out the bonds and close the deal. They arrange instead to renew the maturing draft. This they do by paying the original ninety-day draft out of the proceeds of a new ninety-day draft.

The original draft for ?0,000 comes due let us say on October 19, so that about October 10th the New York banker will be under the necessity of sending over to London a demand draft for ?0,000. The rate realizable for ninety-day drafts being always considerably lower than the price of demand drafts, it follows that if the banker proposes to buy ?0,000 of demand out of the proceeds of a fresh ninety-day bill he will have to draw his fresh bill for more than ?0,000. If the demand rate happened to be 4.86, the ?0,000 he needs would cost him $243,000. In order to raise $243,000 by selling a ninety-days' sight draft (say at 4.83) he would have to make the new draft for ?0,310. The extra ?10 would constitute the interest. Each time he renewed the draft he would have to draw for more and more.

Requiring the tying up of no actual capital, this form of financing "floating investments" has become exceedingly popular and is carried on on a large scale. Where the relationships between the foreign and the American houses are close, there is almost no limit to the number of times an original bill may be renewed. As for the constantly increasing amount of the drafts which have to be drawn, that is taken care of by the interest on the investment carried.

Not all the floating investment in American securities is carried in this way, but in whatever form the financing is done it is bound to involve foreign exchange operations and to necessitate the drawing of drafts by banking houses in this country on their correspondents abroad. Quiet conditions may result in long periods when investments of this kind are left undisturbed, but even then, the constant remitting and renewing of drafts originates a good deal of exchange market activity. And with considerable frequency occur periods when the floating investment is strongly affected by immediate conditions, and when purchases, sales, and transfers of securities stir the exchange market to a high pitch of excitement.

Speculative operations in this market for foreign account, are, however, the cause of the greatest amount of exchange market activity caused by international security transactions. There are times, as has been said, when individuals and banking houses abroad speculate heavily and continuously in this market, at which times the exchange market is strongly affected by the buying and selling of exchange which necessarily takes place. Such periods may last for weeks or even months, and during all of the time, London's immediate attitude toward the market is apt to be the controlling influence on the movement of exchange rates.

Concerning arbitraging in stocks, operations of this kind will be found to divide themselves readily into two classes--trades which are closed off at both ends at once, and trades which are allowed to run over night or even for a day or two. The former is a class of business out of which a dozen or twenty well-equipped houses in New York are making a great deal of money. With an expert "at the rail" on the floor of the New York Stock Exchange, and continuous quotations as to prices on the various stock exchanges in Europe coming in, these houses are in a position to take advantage of the slightest disparity in prices. The chance to buy a hundred shares of some stock, in London, for instance, and to sell it out at the same time in New York, at one-eighth or one-quarter more, is what the arbitrageurs are constantly on the lookout for. With the proper facilities, an expert, in the course of the hour during which the London and New York Stock Exchanges are simultaneously in session, is often able to put through a number of profitable trades.

Such operations are possible, primarily, because of the fact that the same influences affect different markets in different ways. A piece of news which might cause a little selling of some stock in London, for instance, might have exactly the opposite effect in New York. With the wires continually hot between the two markets and a number of experts on the watch for the chance to make a fraction, quotations here and abroad can hardly get very far apart, at least in the active issues, but occasionally, it does happen that the arbitrageur is able to take advantage of a substantial difference. Always without risk, the bid in one market being in hand before the stock is bought in the other market.

But not so in the case of the other kind of arbitrage, where stocks bought in one market are carried over night for the sake of selling them out in some other market the next morning. There a decided risk is taken, the success of the operation depending absolutely upon the judgment of the operator. Under the stimulus of some favorable development, for instance, which becomes known here only after the Stock Exchanges abroad are closed for the day, the New York market closes buoyant. The chances are that the receipt of the news abroad over night will make the London market open up strong in the morning. To buy stock right at the closing of the market here for the purpose of selling it out next morning in London at the opening is an operation not without risk, but one which is likely to make money. A lower opening abroad would, of course, spoil the whole plan, and force a loss, but just there comes in the ability and judgment of the man who is handling the business. His judgment need by no means be infallible for the house to make a great deal of money.

Concerning arbitraging in bonds, practically everything depends not only on the judgment and skill, but on the facilities and connections of the man in charge. In the great "open" market in New York and in the great "open" market in London, American bonds are being continually bid for and offered in a way which gives an expert in touch with both markets a chance to buy here and sell there, or vice versa, at a profit. Such men are employed by bond houses with international connections, and spend their time doing practically nothing else but keeping in close touch with open market bids and offers for stocks and bonds and trying to buy in one market and sell in another. Such trades are frequently put through on a very profitable basis, profits of a clear point or more being not at all uncommon.

As for the degree of risk to be taken in business of this kind, that is entirely at the discretion of the arbitrageur. Where a firm bid of ninety-nine, good for the day, for instance, is given, there is no risk in cabling a bid of ninety-eight to London, but where the bid is not firm at all, or where it is only firm for five minutes, or in many other cases, the man who cables his own bid of ninety-eight is taking a certain amount of risk. Often enough he gets the bonds in London at ninety-eight, only to find that the ninety-nine bid in New York has been withdrawn.

Knowledge of what risks to take and of what risks to leave alone constitutes expertness in this line of business. Seldom can the transaction be absolutely closed at both ends and any substantial profit be made. Most of the time the correctness of the bond expert's judgment as to how he can sell somewhere else what he has bought, is what determines the amount of money he will make or lose.

CHAPTER IX

THE FINANCING OF EXPORTS AND IMPORTS

Interesting as the movement of gold and the international money markets may be, it is in its application to the every-day importing and exporting of merchandise that foreign exchange has its greatest interest for the greatest number of people. Every bale of cotton exported from the country, every pound of coffee brought in, is the basis of an operation in foreign exchange, such operations involving usually the issue of what is known as "commercial credits."

Broadly speaking, commercial credits are of two classes, those issued to facilitate the import of merchandise and those issued to facilitate its export. Considering the question from the standpoint of New York, import credits are so much more important than export credits and issued in so much larger volume, they will be taken up first.

Not all the merchandise imported into the United States is brought in under commercial letters of credit, but that is coming to be more and more the way in which payment for imports is being arranged. Formerly an importer who had bought silk or white-goods in France went around to his banker, bought a draft on Paris for the required amount of francs and sent that over in payment. In some cases that is still the method by which payment is made, but in the very great majority of cases where the business is being run on an up-to-date basis, a commercial letter of credit is arranged for before the importation is made. Of how great advantage such an arrangement is to the merchant importing goods the following practical illustration of how a "credit" works will show.

[Illustration: Form of Commercial Letter of Credit]

To exemplify the greatest number of points of importance possible in connection with the commercial credit business, the case of a shipment of raw silk from China will, perhaps, serve best. A silk manufacturer in Paterson, New Jersey, we will assume, has purchased by cable ten bales of raw silk in Canton, China. Understanding of the successive steps in the financing of such a transaction will mean a pretty satisfactory understanding of the general principles under which the financing of most of our imports is arranged.

The purchase of the silk having been consummated by cable, the first thing the purchaser would do would be to go to his banker in New York, lay before him an exact statement of the conditions under which the purchase was made, and get him (the banker) to open a commercial letter of credit covering those terms. Such a credit, of which a reprint is given herewith, would be in the form of a letter to the issuing banker's London correspondent, requesting him to "accept" the drafts of the sellers of the silk in Canton up to a certain amount and under certain conditions. These conditions, having to do with the "usance" of the drafts (whether they were to be drawn at three, four, or six months' sight) and with the shipping documents to accompany the drafts, are all very fully set forth in the letter of credit itself. If the silk has been bought on the basis of four months, for instance, the credit would read that drafts are to be drawn at four months' sight. Mention is also made as to whose order the bills of lading are to be made, as to where the insurance is to be effected, etc., etc.

The silk importer having received this letter of credit from the banker in New York, sends it by first mail (or, if the case be urgent, cables its contents) to the seller of the silk out in Canton. The latter, having received it, is then in a position to go ahead with his shipment. The first thing he does is to put the silk aboard ship, receiving from the steamship company a receipt (bill of lading) stating that the ten bales have been put aboard, and making them deliverable to the order of the banker in New York, who issues the credit. The bill of lading being made out to his order is useless to anybody else. He and he only can get the silk out of the ship when it arrives in New York.

The shipper in Canton having received this bill of lading from the steamship company and having properly insured the goods and received a certificate stating that he has done so, is then in a position to go ahead and draw his draft for the cost of the silk. The London correspondent of the New York banker, to whom the letter of credit is addressed, is, say, the Guaranty Trust Company of London. Upon that institution the Canton silk firm, therefore, draws his draft in pounds sterling for the cost of the silk, attaching to the draft the bill of lading, an invoice, and the insurance certificate.

A pertinent inquiry at this point is as to why the letter of credit for silk shipped from a city in China directs that drafts be drawn on London--as to why London figures in the transaction at all? The answer is that drafts on London are always readily negotiable, and that London is the only city in the whole world drafts on which are readily negotiable in all places and at all times. A draft on New York or on Berlin might be negotiated at a point like Canton, but to be sure that the exporter of the silk will get the best rate of exchange for his drafts, the drafts must be drawn on London, the financial center of the world. One of the chief points to the whole business of taking out a credit, in fact, is to provide a point on which the shipper can draw satisfactorily.

Assume now that the silk has been put aboard ship bound for the United States, that the shipper has drawn, say, a draft for ?,000 at four months' sight on the Guaranty Trust Co., London, and has attached thereto the bill of lading and the insurance certificate. Taking this draft around to his bank the shipper sells it for local currency at the then prevailing rate for four months' sight drafts drawn on London. The fact that it is drawn at four months' sight means that he will get a lower rate of exchange for it than if it were drawn payable on demand, but that was the arrangement with the buyer in New York--that the drafts against the silk were to have four months to run.

Having sold this draft to his bank in Canton and received local currency therefor, the shipper of the silk is out of the transaction. He has shipped the goods and he has his money. What becomes of the draft he drew is the next important point to consider. But so far as the exporter is concerned, the transaction is closed, and he is ready for the next operation.

The silk has now been set afloat for New York, and the draft purchased by the Canton banker is on its way to London for acceptance. Long before the silk gets to New York the draft will have reached London and will have been presented to the cashier of the Guaranty Trust Co., there, who, of course, was apprised of the credit opened on his bank at the time such credit was originally issued in New York. Examining the draft and the documents carefully to see that they conform with the terms of the credit, the cashier of the Guaranty Trust Co., London, formally "accepts" the draft, marking it payable four months from the date it was presented to him. The accepted draft he hands back to the messenger of the bank who brought it in; the bill of lading, insurance certificate, and invoice he keeps. By the next mail steamer he dispatches these papers to the banker in New York who issued the credit.

For the time being, at least, that is to say, till the accepted draft comes due, the London banker is out of the transaction, which is now narrowed down to the importer of the silk in Paterson and the banker in New York who issued him the credit.

Assume now that a week has passed and that the New York banker finds himself in possession of a bill of lading for ten bales of silk, merchandise deliverable to his order. A few days later, perhaps, the goods arrive overland by fast freight from Seattle. The Paterson silk manufacturer, who is eagerly awaiting their arrival, comes around to the banker: "Endorse over the bill of lading to me," he says, "so that I can get the silk and start manufacturing it."

If the banker does it, he will be giving over the only security he has for the payment at maturity of the draft his London correspondent accepted, and for which he himself is responsible. Still, the manufacturer has to have his silk.

A number of different agreements exist between bankers and importers to whom the bankers issue credits, as to the terms on which the importers are to be allowed to take possession of the merchandise when it arrives here. Sometimes the goods are put into store and handed over to the merchant only when he shows that he has sold them and needs them to make delivery. Sometimes they are warehoused at once, and parcelled out to the importer only in small lots, as he needs them. But more often the goods are delivered over to the importer on his signing one form or other of what is known as a "trust receipt."

Such difference of opinion exists among foreign exchange men as to the goodness of the trust receipt system that the author refrains from making comment on it, confining himself strictly to description of what the system is. As will be seen from the accompanying reprint of the trust receipt used by one of the largest issuers of commercial credits in the country, the document is simply a pledge on the part of the importer to hold the merchandise in trust for the banker, and, as the merchandise is sold, to hand over the proceeds to apply against the draft drawn by the shipper of the goods. The theory of the thing is that by the time all the merchandise has been sold more than enough money will have been handed over to the New York banker to take care of the draft accepted by his London correspondent, the excess constituting the importer's profit.

The kind of trust receipt under which bankers are willing to give over the merchandise (the only collateral they have) naturally varies according to the standing of the house in question. In the case of some importers the bankers would be willing to let the bill of lading pass out of their hands on almost any kind of a receipt; in the case of others a very strict and binding contract is invariably signed. But whatever the form of the contract, it is to be borne in mind that when the banker issuing the credit hands over the bill of lading to the importer on trust receipt, he is allowing the only security he has to pass out of his hands, and is putting himself in the position of having made an unsecured loan to the importer.

Returning now to the particular transaction in question, the point has been reached where the silk is in the importer's hands, that result having been accomplished without the importer having put up a cent of money. Moreover, for nearly four months to come there will be no necessity of the importer's putting up any money (unless he should sell some of the silk, in which case he is bound to turn over the money to the New York banker as a "prepayment"). But in the ordinary course of events the importer of the silk has nearly the four full months in which to fabricate the goods and sell them. At the end of that time the draft drawn by the firm in Canton and accepted by the Guaranty Trust Co., London, will be coming due, and the silk importer will be under the necessity of remitting funds to meet it. Twelve days before the actual maturity of the ?,000 draft in London, the New York banker will send to the manufacturer in Paterson a memorandum for ?,000 at, say, 4.86 (whatever is the current rate) plus commission. The silk firm pays in dollars; the New York banker uses the dollars to buy a demand draft for ?,000; a day or two before the four months' sight draft comes due in London this demand draft ("cover") is received in London from New York, and the whole operation is closed.

It has been deemed advisable to set forth the whole course of one of these import-financing transactions, in order that each successive step may be clearly understood. The question of just why this credit business is worked as it is will now be taken up.

The whole purpose of the business, it is plain enough, is to give the importer here a chance to bring in goods without putting up any actual money--in other words, of letting him use a larger capital than he is actually possessed of. There are persons so conservative as to consider this in itself a wrong idea, but with business carried on along the lines on which it is actually done nowadays, bank credits play so important a part that conservatism of this order has little place. Theory and practice prove that there is no reason why a silk importer, for instance, with a capital of $100,000 should not be able to use safely a credit of as much more than that, the standing and credit of the firm being always the prime consideration. Granted that a manufacturer stands well and is doing a safe, non-speculative business on the basis of $100,000 capital, there is no reason why he should not be able to secure an import credit for an additional ?0,000. Not only is there no reason why he should not get it, but there are any number of good banking concerns only too glad to furnish it to him.

So much for the transaction from the importer's standpoint--what does the seller of the goods get out of it? Payment for his goods as soon as he is ready to ship them. No waiting for a remittance, no drawing of a dollar-draft on an obscure firm in Paterson, N.J., which no Canton bank will be willing to buy at any price. The credit constitutes authority for the shipper to draw in pounds sterling on London--the one kind of draft which he can always be sure of turning at once into local currency and at the most favorable rate of exchange. He ships the goods, he draws the draft, he sells the draft, he has his money, and he is out of it. From the shipper's standpoint, surely a most satisfactory arrangement and one which will induce him to quote the very best price for merchandise.

As to the banker's part in the transaction, the whole question is one of commission. The London banker on whom the credit is issued gets a commission from the American banker for "accepting" the drafts, and the American banker, of course, gets a substantial commission from the party to whom the credit is issued. Sometimes the banker in New York and the banker in London work on joint-account, in which case both risk and commissions are equally divided. But more often, perhaps, the London bank gets such-and-such a fixed commission for accepting drafts drawn under credits, and the New York banker keeps the rest of what he makes out of the importer.

Before proceeding with discussion of what commissions amount to, it is well to note the fact that in those commercial credit transactions neither banker is ever under the necessity of putting up a cent of actual money. As in the case of foreign loans previously described, the banker's credit and the banker's credit only is the basis of the whole operation. The London bank never pays out any actual cash--it merely "accepts" a four months' sight draft, knowing that before the draft comes due and is presented at its wicket for payment, "cover" will have been provided from New York. The New York banker, on the other hand, merely sends over on account of the maturing draft in London the money he receives from the importer. He is under an obligation to the London banker to see that the whole ?,000 is paid off before the four months are over, but he knows the party to whom he issued the credit, and knows that before that time all the silk will have been manufactured and sold and the proceeds turned over to him. At no time is he out of any actual cash.

That being the case, the amount of commission he charges is really very moderate--one-quarter of one per cent. for each thirty days of the life of drafts drawn under credits being the "full rate." Under such an arrangement an importer taking a credit stipulating that the drafts are to be drawn at thirty days' sight would have to pay one-quarter of one per cent.; at sixty days' sight, one-half of one per cent.; at ninety days' sight, three-quarters of one per cent., etc. Such commission to be collected at the time the drafts drawn under the credits fall due.

These are the "full rates"--naturally, few importers are required to pay them, actual rates being largely a matter of individual negotiation and standing. Where the drafts under the credits run for ninety days, for instance, as in the case of coffee imported from Brazil, the full rate would be three-quarters of one per cent., but very few firms actually pay over three-eighths of one per cent. Similarly with credits issued for the importation of merchandise of almost every other kind. Silk credits, with drafts running four months, ought at the regular rate to cost one per cent.; but as a matter of fact there are any number of good houses willing to do the business for five-eighths of one per cent. One large international bank in New York, indeed, is going so far as to offer to issue credits under which drafts run six months for a commission of five-eighths of one per cent. Such a commission is entirely inadequate and no fair compensation for the trouble and risk the banker takes. It means little more than that the bank is willing to take business at any price for advertising or other purposes.

Assume that an importer has taken out a ninety-day credit and is to pay three-eighths of one per cent. on all drafts drawn thereunder, what rate of interest is he actually paying, figured on an annual basis? The life of the draft is ninety days, and he pays three-eighths of one per cent.; in each year there are four ninety-day periods; figured on an annual basis, therefore, the importer is paying four multiplied by three-eighths of one per cent., equalling one and one-half per cent. interest. Not a very high charge, and made possible only because the banker lends his credit and not his cash.

For purposes of illustration, the financing of the import of silk from China was chosen because the operation embodied perhaps more points of interest in connection with commercial credit business than any other one operation. Commercial credit operations, however, are of great variety and scope. They may involve, for instance, the import of matting shipped from Japan on slow sailing ships and where the drafts drawn run for six months or more, or they may involve the import of dress goods from France, in which case the drafts are often at sight. Furthermore, all credits are by no means issued on London. In the Far East, where tea or shellac or silk is being exported to the United States, London is known as the one great commercial and financial center, but in the case of dress goods shipped from Marseilles or Lyons, for instance, the credits would invariably stipulate that the drafts be drawn in francs on Paris.

But whether the material imported be dress goods from France or tea from China, the principle of the commercial credits under which the goods are brought in remains identically the same. In every case there is a buyer on this end who wants to get possession of the goods without having to put up any money, and in every case there is a seller on the other end who wants to receive payment as soon as he lets the merchandise get out of his hands. The banker issuing the credit is merely the intermediary, and the naming of some foreign point on which the drafts are to be drawn is merely incidental to the conduct of the operation.

One last point remains to be cleared up. The seller of the goods in the silk-importing operation described gets actual money for the goods as soon as he ships them--where does this actual money come from? In the last analysis, from the discount market in London, from the man in London who discounts the draft after it has been "accepted". The exporter in Canton gets the money direct from his banker in Canton, but the latter is willing to let him have the money in exchange for the draft only because he (the banker) knows that he can send the draft to London and that some one there will eagerly discount it. In that way the Canton banker gets his money back. The only party who is out of any money during the time the silk is being manufactured and sold in Paterson, N.J., is the party in London who has discounted the shipper's draft.

The real function of the banker, then, in these Commercial Credit transactions is to open up the international loaning market to the importer. Through the system now in force this is accomplished by a banker in New York issuing a credit and by a banker in London putting his "acceptance" on drafts drawn under that credit. The combination makes the drafts good; makes the great discount market in London willing to take them, and absorb them, and advance real money on them. And for the opening up of this great reservoir of capital the importer here has to pay an interest rate of but from one to two per cent. per

###